I am your

JESUS of MERCY

Volume V

I am your

JESUS of MERCY

Volume V

Queenship
PUBLISHING COMPANY
P.O Box 42028 Santa Barbara, CA 93140-2028
(800) 647-9882 • (805) 957-4893 • Fax: (805) 957-1631

The publisher recognizes and accepts that the final authority regarding these apparitions and messages rests with the Holy See of Rome, to whose judgement we willingly submit.

– The Publisher

©1996 Queenship Publishing

Library of Congress Number # 96-87010

Published by:
  Queenship Publishing
  P.O. Box 42028
  Santa Barbara, CA 93140-2028
  (800) 647-9882 • (805) 957-4893 • Fax: (805) 957-1631

Printed in the United States of America

ISBN: 1-882972-74-0

Contents

PUBLISHER'S NOTE

A question most frequently asked of the seer, Gianna Talone-Sullivan has been: "What does Our Lady, the Blessed Mother Mary, the Mother of God look like?"

In early 1995 after previously attending Our Lady's Prayer Group at St. Joseph's Roman Catholic Church in Emmitsburg, Maryland, Peter V. Bianchi approached visionary Gianna Talone-Sullivan with a desire to paint Our Lady as she has seen her for the last eight years.

We give you this inspirational picture that Peter attributes to Our Lady and not himself. Following ten months of intense collaboration with Gianna, this beautiful image is the fruit of her helping the artist to get a likeness of the Holy Mother as she sees her.

Peter is a lifelong artist from the Washington D.C. area, working many years for *National Geographic Magazine*. His desire is that we all delight in this beautiful portrait, to meditate on the messages of Our Lady of Emmitsburg and to be open to Her guidance leading us to holiness.

FOREWARD

Fr. Alfred R. Pehrsson, C.M.
Pastor, St. Joseph's Catholic Church
Emmitsburg, MD

"Bless Me, Father, I'm Jewish!"

In the spring of '95 I had been hearing confessions for more than an hour in our parish church of St. Joseph's, Emmitsburg, Maryland, during the time of Eucharistic adoration on Thursday. I had been a priest for 37 years, but this was the first time I had ever heard, "Bless me, Father, I'm Jewish."

The penitent continued, "I am a Jewish doctor from a nearby state. My wife is also a Jewish doctor. She is outside in the church. We come here often. We have an ethical problem, and this is the only way I could speak with you this afternoon." After we talked for a few minutes, he thanked me for our conversation, asked for a blessing, and added, "Father, this Jewish Mother of yours is really getting to us. Mary has led us to Jesus. We will be Catholics someday."

Isn't this the continuing maternal role of the Blessed Mother in the world today? At Cana of Galilee, didn't she direct the waiters to "Do whatever He tells you to do"? In this moment of time Mary is saying the same words of direction, "Listen and do!" What Jesus is telling us to do is to welcome His merciful love.

In this latest volume of "**I am your JESUS of MERCY,**" dictating to Gianna Talone-Sullivan, Jesus is calling Jew and Gentile to return to the Father. The role of the merciful Jesus is to bring all people back to God the Father through the power of the Holy Spirit as soon as possible. He accomplishes this as the Lord who so willingly forgives, encourages, and consoles us as the "Jesus of Mercy."

Divine Mercy is Divine Love in action. It comes from the treasury of the Sacred Heart of the Savior. Mercy calls for union with God from whom we all have come and to whom we all one day will return. With mercy comes the assurance of certainty of victory over the evil one. With mercy comes the peace that surpasses all understanding. Repentant for past offenses and with those sins "forgiven, forgotten, forever," we prayerfully meditate on that future day when we will stand before the all-knowing Judge. At that moment we will ask Him to kindly remember the many times in our lives when we asked for loving mercy. He won't forget. He's got a good memory!

Gianna Talone-Sullivan and her husband are parishoners of St. Joseph's in Emmitsburg, home parish of St. Elizabeth Ann Seton. Is the Lord speaking messages of mercy to the world through Gianna? I believe He is. Having known this well-balanced, good-humored doctor for two years, I have concluded that Gianna is a chosen instrument in the hands of Our Lord and Our Lady. She truly knows Our Lord and Our Lady. She lives intimately with them day by day.

Our Christian faith teaches us that the Gospel writings are the inspired words of God and the principle sources of revelation and meditation on the mercy of God. However, Jesus is God! He has limitless ways of reaching us. In recent times, through chosen people, He continues to remind us that "I am your Jesus of Mercy." Paraphrasing the words of the Jewish doctor in Emmitsburg, may we all say: "Bless me, Father,... I am in need of your mercy."

PART I

Lessons 1-30

November 1994 - November 1995

Lessons received through
Gianna Talone-Sullivan

Lesson #1
At Villa St. Michael in front of the Blessed Sacrament
November 11,1994

THE LOVE OF THE FATHER

My dear little one, I your Lord love you and give to you My Most Sacred Heart in which to rest. I betroth to you My Mother who is the Mediatrix of all graces and good cheer. My little one, I wish for My people to know that I am in their midst at all times, but in a very real way in My Most Blessed Sacrament. I invite all My people to raise their hearts to God the Father through My Blessed Sacrament. When you come before Me, be at peace. Rest in My love. Put aside all distractions, fear, worry and concern. Realize you are before Me and contemplate My love and goodness. If you will absorb My love and rest in My love, your heart, mind, and soul will be rejuvenated and will rise to an ectasy of joy. When you rest in My Heart, a peace overcomes you, almost a state of sleep; but you are resting truly in My Most Sacred Heart where I am carrying you and sifting through all your needs and organizing all your spiritual and temporal needs for the glory of God the Father.

I love you, little one, and I love all My people. I invite all to be "little". When you are "little", the Father is able to embrace your soul ever so tightly and He will protect you. Nothing is able to slip by Him without His blessing and knowledge. Therefore you can be sure of safety and protection in His love. How My Father desires to be the tender Father of all My people. They will not allow Him because many are so fearful of Him and have kept their distance. Many are lacking the knowledge of His tender love and kindness and have ignored His calling of peace. Therefore, many people restrict the graces and good fortunes designated for them. O' how the love pours forth from His rays of light. Tell My people, my little one, of His love and invite all to a new light of truth, free of confusion.

Here I am before you in My Most Blessed Sacrament commencing the next set of lessons for My people. Elevate your soul in My love. Put aside all fear, worry and distractions. Rest in My love. Rest in My peace. Rest in Me as I rest in you. Let us unite for we are ONE.

Little one, you thought I had forgotten you because you have not heard My words and lessons for My people for two years, but I have not forgotten. If all would forget you, I would not forget you. It is the same for all My people. What is two years in the timetable of man that in God's time cannot be fulfilled in a matter of minutes? It is time now to take My words for My people. I bless you and I love you. Know that it is not that I was ignoring you. It was not the time in God's timetable that I continue. I was always with you as I am with you now. Contemplate these words of Mine and ponder them in your heart! Peace. AD DEUM.

Lesson #2
At Villa St. Michael in front of the Blessed Sacrament
November 25, 1994

THE POWER OF THE CHILDREN

My dear little one, PEACE is with you. I am PEACE. I am the WAY, the TRUTH and the LIFE. In ME all good things come. In ME all life exists. I am LOVE. Without LOVE life ceases to exist.

Today, little one, I wish to speak of the Eternal Father's love and the power which belongs to the children of the world. It is in their innocence, their purity and their weakness that the power of God lives. The salvation of humanity shall come through the little children. The Eternal Father responds and hears the cries of His children. It was through the "yes" of My Mother that the Church was born. It is through the "yes" of the little children that the salvation of humanity shall come and peace will exist. The little children hold great power in their "littleness".

Tell all the little children they are invited to be instruments of My peace. Form an army with nests of prayer. Be consecrated to My Mother's Immaculate Heart which will triumph. Pray in your families, neighborhoods, and privately. Do little penances for the Father in love, and adore the Holy Trinity through devotion to the most Blessed Sacrament. I wish to make it clear that all My children are invited to belong to Me. My Father awaits their love. I invite all parents to encourage My little children to pray and to love. Teach your little ones in My love to avoid all things that would cause confusion or foster violence. I need you My dear loved ones, the parents of My little children. Do you not see that it is the children who can save the world through their little ways, their purity, innocence, simpleness, prayers, and weakness? My Father takes the little ones, the pure ones, the weak ones, the innocent ones, and gives them power to do great works through their prayers and simple little ways. He makes it clear that His grace is fulfilled. The little children work for the glory of God, not their own glory. They are forgiving and totally dependent on His care. My Father never fails to respond to any little child who cries out to Him. The sweetness of the Eternal Father lovingly caresses in His bosom all the little children of the world and nourishes them. He is NOT a fearful, distant Father. He is loving, tender, and filled with love. He desires to give to His children.

Have the children pray for the sick, the lonely, the persecuted, the poor and the broken hearted. Have the little children pray for peace. They are hungry for love and will be filled with the suckling milk of God the Father. The little children are searching. Introduce them to His love. Their "yes" will open the heavens, and rays of light and graces will pour forth. My Mother will care for them and teach them in their "yes" how to prepare for battle; and the little children will fight the death of evil and be victorious in their "yes" through their love, penance, littleness, purity, and innocence. As the battle was once engaged in the heavens and the angel Lucifer was cast out from the heavens, so too will the battle again engage; and if they say "yes", the children will be victorious, casting out the death of evil.

Invite the children to PEACE. Invite all My children. My Father is waiting for their "yes". The heavens are waiting to be opened by the little children of the world. In gaining peace they will save humanity. AD DEUM.

Lesson #3
At Villa St. Michael, Exposition of the Blessed Sacrament
December 2, 1994

THE SEED OF LOVE

My dear little one, I desire My people to come to Me, to take time for Me, to slow down and move at a pace which allows them to absorb the goodness of My Father present in everything. It is necessary to nurture and cultivate the seed of love infused by the Father. How do you nurture the seed planted by Love? Your desire to allow the seed to grow and blossom opens the aquaducts of Love to water and feed the soul.

My Father instills in you Love. His goodness draws your will to Love. He draws your intellect to ponder Him in contemplation. Everything which is good comes from the Father. You could not love if the Father did not will it. You could not love Him if He did not draw you to Himself. Therefore, in contemplation you gain admiration and devotion to His Love. His works of love are not founded only on prayer and admiration but in deeds. What fruit in love is there without action and charity? My Father gave Love to you. If He draws you to Love and you keep it to yourself it will die. The seed of love must be nurtured and watered through action. The fruit will not blossom unless the soil is tilled and watered. So too is it with love. If you have fidelity in love to the Father, you have not only contemplation and admiration but acts of charity in deeds.

It is necessary to realize that your weaknesses and imperfections are not driven away, because they are the fuel to sprouting the fruit of humility and chasing the Love of the Father. In your weaknesses you remember you are nothing without Love, and it is the Father who deepens Love in you. You chase after Him desiring to belong totally to Him, to live in total union with Him. Your heart longs for Love. You no longer want only the blessings of God, but you crave God Himself. God is all of yours, and now you ask when will you be all of God's. O' the wonder of Love, to desire to belong to God totally!

I desire that My people slow to a pace of contemplation and admiration of LOVE, love of the Father. No one knows the Father except the Son and whoever the Son chooses to reveal the Father. I desire to introduce the Father to all those who desire "LOVE". I am Love. I am One with the Father. I am yours. Will you be Mine? Will you allow Me to bring you to My sweet loving Father? Once you know the Father you will never desire anything other than what Love desires. I bless you, little one, and I bless all My people. Peace. AD DEUM.

Lesson #4
In private chapel at home
January 6, 1995

LOVE OF GOD IS LOVE OF NEIGHBOR

My little one, My love for you will never cease. My love for My people will never cease. I carry the wounds in My Most Sacred Heart from all the division and wicked ways so many have chosen to pursue. But in My love I will never turn from them, for My door is open to all who desire to enter. It is My people who cease to grow in My love and cease loving Me. They are imperfect in love and grow slack in their journey when they cease to love their neighbor and render service to them. When you withdraw charity from your neighbor because there is no consolation for your own profit, your love is impure. The amount of love you share with your neighbor through charity and unconditonal service is proportional to the amount of love you have for Me. To have the treasure of eternal life in Me your love must be pure.

I love all unconditonally and reward each according to their labor of love. Do you not see, little one, that virtues are developed through openness and unconditional charity to one another? Few arrive at the optimum perfection of love because they first seek self-love and give only as a result of what they can receive in return. How blessed are those who desire Me by giving unconditionally to their neighbor the charity and love so much needed. Blessed are those who do not seek self-love but self-knowledge in the truth of My Divinity. Blessed are those who venture in My love, risking all entities beneficial to themselves without seeking consolation in return. These are My people who trust in My Divine Mercy and humbly submit to My Will. I have so much to give but few who will truly remain faithful to Me without turning away. Many desire Me but then close the door to their hearts when opportunities do not prove profitable for them.

Little one, today in My lesson to My people I want them to know that the amount of love they render in charity to their neighbor is the amount of love they have for Me. Ponder My Words and recognize your position with your neighbor. Evaluate your self-love which consists of conditions, and strive to love as I am Love. Practice! Purity of heart rises from unconditional service and charity. Perfection of love will become the gem which will brighten the path to the throne of God the Father. Peace, little one. My love to My beloved People. AD DEUM.

Lesson #5
In private chapel at home
January 27, 1995

MY PATH TO FREEDOM

My dear one, the days have come when man ("man" is both male and female gender) walks a path of his choice and liking. There are many paths which cross, but only one path which leads to My Kingdom. There is no distinction from one path to another unless you are on My path. Only then will you know the Way. I desire all My people to choose My path, but the road seems too narrow for them. They desire wider paths and more space in rushing for freedom. They do not realize the freedom they are racing to grasp can only be found on the pathway to My Father's Kingdom.

I have long since been reaching out to My beloved people in very intimate ways, making known the truth of My Presence and protection, but few truly capture the essence of My love. Why is this? (Jesus asked me to respond.) Yes, little one, it is because they are afraid. They do not trust in My words. How can they take delight in the Word when they do not trust in the Word? I have told them, "Be not afraid, I am with you always"; but these are merely words to them, not reality. They do not see Me with their eyes, and consequently they make opinionated remarks and conclusions that I have abandoned them. What the eyes do not see, the soul sees. It is faith in God that permits you to trust. Faith is a grace which is given to My people by the Holy Spirit. Faith, however, is not practiced in the fervor of love. Blessed are they who believe and do not see. Pray for a deepening of your faith in order that you will gain trust in Me. Do you not know that all things are possible with God? Why then do you limit your opportunity to grow and attain great achievements through your lack of trust? Trust in Me. Be not afraid. You do not understand that which is Divine and therefore cannot comprehend the depth and breadth of My Presence at your side at all times. Place your confidence in Me. This is your choice in selecting which pathway to walk. Choose the path of faith, trust, and confidence. This path is the pathway to freedom. My path is not narrow except for those who through their desire to control and their fear have placed their own limitations and restrictions which narrow the dimensions of My path. This results in them selecting an alternate path instead of Mine. I love all My people, little one. All are special to Me. All are accounted for in My love. There can be tremendous progress for all who make the decision to trust and utilize their faith.

My dear one, I am with you. I want to see all My people take delight in the Word, for I am the Word. If you love Me, you will love also your neighbor. How can you love your neighbor if you do not take delight in the Word? Study the Word. Know the Word and you will know the passion of fidelity and true love. The more you take delight in God, the more you will receive, for the more you surrender and are willing to receive. Delight in the Word through the eyes of your soul. Be refreshed in My love. Be comforted through your trust and faith in Me. Be rewarded with the Kingdom of God on the path which leads to the Divine Gates of Heaven. I bless you, little one, and all people, with the blessing of My Father. Peace to you all. Peace. AD DEUM.

Lesson #6
In private chapel at home
February 6, 1995

THE OPPORTUNITY OF KNOWLEDGE AND WISDOM

My dear little one, I your Lord God am merciful. I have not dealt harshly with My people as in the days of old when Moses proclaimed My covenant to My people. They were a wicked generation not willing to follow My way and change their stone hearts from evil ways. I have made a new covenant with My people through the sacrifice of My life in order that they would be saved from final damnation. I have told My people that I am a merciful God and that I want repentant hearts. I have kept My promise from past ages of leading My people out from exile to the land of milk and honey. I have protected My people, clothed them, fed them, and I have walked among them. Why do so many of My people turn from Me and choose the comforts of this world instead of the long-lasting eternal comforts? They continue to show Me their disinterest in knowing Me. They have no desire for the opportunity to grow in knowledge, wisdom, compassion or charity. Their desires are short-lived in momentary pleasures of self. They have forsaken Me. How long should this continue before I hide My face from them and close the heavens?

My faithful people, by the light of their holy faith, have rekindled the darkness to light. They offer Me the sacrifice of justice with holy lives. They are the pearls of My mercy through their upright and holy lives. They render Me glory and praise, despising vice and embracing virtue. These, My beloved people, through their desire to grow in the opportunity of knowledge and wisdom, are the soothing balm on My most broken heart. By living virtuously, they cauterize the wound of sin in the world, giving Me honor for the salvation of souls. They do not think of themselves, but of My honor. Their service is unconditional. These are My people, where in My garden they dwell. Their actions are the peace and light in the minds of all people. For My faithful ones have upheld My Holy Church.

My people with indifference and disinterest in correcting their sin continue to act like blind ones, pretending not to see their ways. They fear of the loss of their position or material goods; and they are deprived of the light of knowledge and of all grace, all because of their lukewarm hearts of indifference and disinterest. They do not correct their faults. They do not attempt to pray unless they receive consolation in return. They do not stand firm in penance, so they are blind and confounded in guilt. My people who are dwelling in My sweet fragrance of mercy do not act as such. They do not fear to correct their ways and ultimately burn in the inextinguishable fire of My love. They are My angels of light.

Make known to My people My truth, little one. Never fear, for I walk amongst you, clothe you, and provide you food to eat. Do not be afraid. I am with you, never to leave you. Tell My people My words. Pray for My people. Bring them to Me in prayer so that none may be lost. Peace, little one. My peace I give to you. Share My peace with all people. I have rested My hand of authority on you. Bring all My people home to My Most Sacred Heart. I bless you. AD DEUM.

Lesson #7
In private chapel at home
March 6, 1995

PRAYER: The Tool of Intimacy

My dear little one, the grace of My Father is shed from His love for you and in His desire for you to be fulfilled in His love. I want all to come to Me in simplicity, seeking a deeper union with Me through prayer. Prayer elevates the mind, heart and soul into the abyss of truth: truth of self-knowledge, truth in humility, truth in obedience, and truth of knowledge of your Savior. My Father bestows His blessing of grace for prayer. All I desire from My people is to have an intimate relationshp with them. I desire for them to come to Me in solicitude and submissiveness. I desire them to come before Me even in their compunction of sin. I just want My people to spend time with Me, to be with Me, to share with Me all their concerns, joys, sorrows and challenges. I desire to be asked for guidance. I desire to be their closest friend. It is through the grace of prayer from My Father that this is possible.

Prayer is the vessel through which love is purified and perfected. It is the tool of intimacy. Take time to listen to My silence. You will find in focusing on Me and listening to My words of love in silence that the business of your thoughts will be tempered in My love. You will find the joy and depth of knowing love through knowledge of yourself. You will know TRUTH. Through continual prayer you will gain the grace of every virtue. It is good to exercise mental prayer in addition to vocal prayer. Meditate and ponder the mystery of love. Pondering My love and My life will give rise to joy in the soul. Prayer removes vice, and vice blinds My people. When your heart is dedicated to My love, it is also dedicated to yourself; for My glory is also yours. Love Me with all your heart and you will be inseparable from Me. When I am adored, you too are honored.

Little one, desire what I desire. Give heed to My grace and respond to My inspirations through prayer. I love you and all My people. I desire to give to all the fruits of truth, love and hope. I am your Savior. I desire to help My loved ones; but they desire not My help, for they continue to place restrictions on their lives by distancing themselves from Me and through their lack of prayer. If you struggle with prayer, ask Me for the grace and I shall come to you. Invite Me to be in your life. I love you and desire you to receive abundantly. Peace, little one. Peace. AD DEUM.

Lesson #8
In private chapel at home
March 18, 1995

THE IDOLATRY OF SELF

My little one, I await the love of My people, but it is conditional. I desire all to come to Me not only during times of need of earthly comfort. So many of My people cannot find the time to rest in My presence of love even for fifteen minutes a day. Their self-interest supercedes the graces which I would like to bestow on them. I desire to care for all My people, and I desire them to come and be with their Friend, their Lover, their Savior. They do not desire to be with Me. They desire instead to nourish their carnal desires over the delights of eternal wisdom, freedom and joy. And so through their free will they limit and obstruct the flow of My grace upon them.

I came to save the sinner, but My people think they have not sinned and do not need God. They have made idols of themselves. Anything which is good within them they display and brag outwardly in self-love. They do not see that all good things come from Me and Me alone, not through their own merit. They consider themselves perfect and in need of no change. Any vice of their flesh is excused. Yet they are impatient with anyone who does not show them respect or honor. They are proud and lack faith. They do not love God and they do not love their countrymen. They thrive on the misfourtunes of their enemies. They are full of pride and self-love. Their lack of faith is due to their negligence in seeking the knowledge of God in truth and in humility. A lack of faith is a lack of conviction about the truth of My sweetness. They do not desire an intimate or personal relationship with Me. They do not desire a deep living faith which surpasses all knowledge. All their intentions stem from self-interest, comfort, and praise about which they boast deceitfully. What state could be more sinful? Yet they think they are not sinners and do not need salvation. This carelessness will result in their own judgment in due season. If they will not heed My Word and allow My mercy to change their strong hearts to repentant hearts, their own judgment standards will toss them into the abyss of eternal flames which will consume their souls in everlasting agony and misery.

My Way is simple, however difficult many might conjecture it to be. I have said many times that I desire to be your Friend. I desire to give you many blessings and fruits from My kingdom. But fear of the unknown and lack of control make it too risky for My people. They do not trust because of their lack of faith. I would deepen their faith, O' if they would allow Me into their hearts. So they do not believe in the Word. If they do not believe, they cannot love, for I am Love. Peace cannot exist unless there is love. How, little one, would you have Me respond to My people who continue to live in a most sinful state? If they continue to transgress My obedience imposed on them, they will become My enemies instead of My people. I redeemed My people through My Blood and restored the life of grace, but they are not grateful. They are obliged to render Me praise and glory. If they continue to deprive Me of glory and continue to claim their glory, the greater will be their offence. For they are not allowing Me to be their God of Mercy.

You restrain Me, little one and all those My beloved ones who seek to love, to serve unconditionally and to appease Me by your tears which bind the punishment of offences through Divine Justice. When you pray for others, My mercy can unfold and the humility of your tears can mitigate the fury of My Father's wrath. Look then to Me for knowledge and truth. Look to Me for fulfillment. I love My people and desire to save their souls which, if left to the hands of mankind alone, will surely die. Pray, little one, for mercy in this world. Tell all My beloved ones to pray for the mercy of God the Father. Peace to you. Peace. AD DEUM.

Lesson #9
In private chapel at home
March 20,1995

THE WONDROUS WORKS OF GOD

My little one, I give My people all the wonders of the world, the morning dew, the chirping birds, the freshness of spring flower blossoms. I desire My people to recognize the beauty and wonders of the earth. Give thanks to God the Father for His love and His creation. Do not take for granted the beauty and simplicity, yet the greatness of the earth's wonders. Open your ears to hear the beauty of life. Open your eyes to see His creation of life. Open your hearts to receive His love and to know His sweetness and His truth. How My Father works in the little small things, the little ones who are dependent on His love.

Have you ever pondered the wondrous works of God? He is so powerful. He desires you to be His glorious people, yet He has no need for you. He has made you little less than a god because of His love for you. You merit nothing at the works of your own hands.

Everything is given to you as a gift from Him. Give praise O' children of Israel to the Father of Mercy whose goodness surpasses all knowledge. Be dependent on Him like little children. He will hold you tight to His loving breast and will protect you against all enemies of hatred. Come to God the Father. His works are awesome and true. His Name is wonderful. He has crowned Me with glory and honor. God the Father is great. He gives life and brings death. He brings healing to many and He inflicts injury on many. He decrees what is necessary to bring the soul to perfection in His love. All His works are wondrous, a sight for the eyes to behold in adoration. Blessed be God the Father! He has given you Me. He is Light without falsehood. In the truth of His love He confounds the devil and destroys his lie so His people can follow the path to His gates of heaven.

Open your hearts My people. Do not follow the father of falsehood, the father of lies. It only leads to the road of damnation. Follow Truth, Love and Peace, the road to heaven. Your safety and security rests in God alone. I love you My people. Come, open your hearts. Seek the Light of Eternal Truth. God refreshes the weary and rewards good deeds of love. Take delight in God. He awaits your love. Peace. AD DEUM.

Lesson #10
In private chapel at home
March 26, 1995

POISONOUS VENOMS OR REFRESHING WATERS?

My dear little one, My children who perform My works of love and mercy are continually judged falsely and are scandalized by others. This is because the poisonous venoms of resentment, jealousy and pride continue to seep into the wicked who thrive on self-love. They judge My beloved ones falsely and attempt to spoil the good fruits of charity. How impure are the motives of those who scandalize the virtuous servants of Mine! How this human generation has become blind to its own dignity! Do you not see that those who are chained to the vices of envy, impatience, jealousy, gossip and hatred, are slaves to sin? They no longer are great but have become small, and are no longer rulers but have become slaves to the prince of darkness. That is why the prince of darkness, Satan, was hurled down from the heavens. His pride and jealousy caused him to boast in self-righteousness and self-love to the point that he would have no glory shared with any human being. He wanted all for himself. From the poison of envy, pride and jealousy grew an incurable hatred which resulted in death.

Those who do not pay heed to My words of love and mercy are deprived of life because they live to sin. But I increase the virtues of mercy and charity in My children. Their torments only increase their graces. Those who judge falsely, however, will live in their own torment, for in the end they will falsely judge their own practices. They will be in misery for they will not allow My mercy to dwell in them. They will judge their sin to be greater than My mercy and will therefore be eternally tormented.

Tell My people My words, little one. It is not My desire that any one person miss the bridge of life and the refreshing waters from which abundant graces flow. I desire all to live in purity and integrity. Know the truth from the deadly effects of sin. To you, My beloved ones, who strive to live in My humility, love and mercy, be not afraid. Your torments will result in your crown of glory which I will share with you. All you who are scandalized, take "courage" as your staff (walking stick) in hand and valiantly conquer the evil of envy with love and perseverance in truth. I am with you always and My Kingdom is yours. All I have I give to you. I bless you, My beloved people. Peace. AD DEUM.

Lesson #11
In private chapel at home
April 30, 1995

REJOICE

My little one, peace be with you. I your Lord God bring you peace for I am Peace. I do not wish for My people to be distraught but to be filled with joy in the Lamb of God. REJOICE and be filled with joy! I am with you. My mercy is upon you and I shall not abandon you. Be at peace. Live in My love. Receive My joy. I tell you that not one shall be lost for all are accounted for by My Father. All My chosen little ones belong to Him. Not one will stray away that My Father will not bring back to Him. Be at peace. Live in charity and love for one another. Rejoice, I am your Lord God, your merciful Savior. Only you can deny yourself My glory by not allowing Me to be merciful. But, all My people have until their last breath to ask for My mercy.

Very few of My people have joy in their Savior. I desire all to come to Me in praise and rejoicing. I do not desire My people to be filled with sorrow or sadness. As I purify and cleanse My people there are emotions and sentiments of self-pity, sadness and sorrow. But I do not want My people to be distraught by these sentiments but instead rejoice, be glad and have hope. The pride must be stripped in order that humility can replace it. It takes time to grow in holiness, charity and love because of human weakness, sinfulness and vices of the flesh. My mercy soothes the pain when My truth lances the flesh of its many vices. Therefore, rejoice in gratitude that you are loved by Me and that you are being purified in order for you to share eternal glory with Me. I love My people beyond their comprehension. Allow your hearts to rest in My love and in My peace, for I am with you. Trust with confidence in My love. Rejoice when you receive ill-treatment for the sake of My Name. You belong to Me. What I have so shall you have. As I have suffered so shall you share in My suffering. Where I am in glory so too shall you share in My glory. Be at peace and rejoice in your Savior's MERCY! Peace to you. AD DEUM.

Lesson #12
In private chapel at home
May 31, 1995

MY JOY

My dear little one, it is with joy that I come to you and My people. I find joy in My beloved people because I love them. The wonder of love fills those who take joy in all they do and encounter each day; joy, because the will of God unfolds as they fulfill their responsibilities in simpleness. The will of God is revealed as you work, pray, encounter and interact with all people. Those who work focusing on the simpleness of My love find joy. I find joy in My people when I look upon families, marriages, children, single lay people, religious, and all men and women who fulfill their daily duties consecrated to the will of God. What joy I have when I see two people as husband and wife consecrated to God in love and simpleness praying together. I find joy in My young ones who do their best in their daily chores, studies, play and prayer. I take joy in My little children, pure of heart and innocent, and in all parents who strive in prayer to live in love and harmony in the family. I find joy in My children who are obedient to their parents in love. The will of God unfolds in all people as they simply remain open, surrendering to love, utilizing all avenues of love which perfect them in holiness. They are filled with joy and peace because they are dedicated to their daily obligations in the littleness and simpleness of My love. Oh, how I am filled with joy in My people. I take delight in them when they desire to fulfill the will of God. I take delight in My religious who dedicate their lives to proclaiming My truth of love. My priests and My religious suffer tremendously as they refuse to follow deception but remain loyal to My current Vicar your Pope and My Church, regardless of any pressure to do otherwise. I find joy in all who are dedicated to My truth at all costs and who are consecrated to My Most Sacred Heart and My Mother's Immaculate Heart. The Two Hearts shall reign in victory and the day will come forth when all the world will know of the triumph of the TWO HEARTS.

I love you, my little child, you who hold the keys for all children to enter the Kingdom of Heaven. I love you. I love all My people as I love you. Blessed be God the Father for His unconditional love and kindness which shower graces upon My people. Blessed be His Holy Name. Find joy in the Father, My beloved ones. He is Love and the Source of Peace. I give you My peace for I give to you all that He has given to Me. Blessings, My people, in unity and oneness of the Triune God. AD DEUM.

Lesson #13
In private chapel at home
July 31, 1995

ALL I CREATED FOR YOU

My dear little one, I love my people and desire all to have a deep peace rooted in the virtues of charity and love. I desire all My people to know Me and to know how much love I have for them and their happiness. It is My desire to give to My people. All is created in this world and orchestrated with great love for them. I am abounding in love. My grace is bountiful. I give My words now in this time period for all My people to know that My love is consistent and will always remain the same. Little one, even if all should forget you, I shall never forget you. I shall always love you and care for you. I shall always remember My people, love them and care for them.

Do not be preoccupied with things and issues of yourself, but focus all attention on your Jesus. I am your Savior. Do not lose the moment by dwelling on a topic regarding yourself. Look to Me and see all the wonders of creation I have set before you. Do not lose the moment by thinking about issues centering around your very self. Just live and be happy in the simplicity of My love. Reflect on all the good and wondrous marvels I created for your happiness. Time in this world continues on with you or without you. Enjoy the time of life in My love. My mercy is endless. Broaden your scope and horizon by focusing on the breadth and depth of My unconditional love, My love for you, My gifts for you, My treasures for you, My mercy for you and My life given in love for you. There is so much that I have given to you and created for you. I want for all souls to be happy. I do not want one soul to be lost. But if you focus on yourself and issues centering around you, you will miss the moment of wondrous gifts set before you and created for you. Broaden your horizons by looking beyond the scope of yourself to that which is Divine. Look to the ocean of My mercy, to the refreshing waters of life, the sounds of encouragement, and to the invitations and challenges to spiritual maturity. All for you, My people, all for you!

I love you and desire you to seek refuge in My Most Sacred Heart, to be safe and happy. Please listen to My words and plea for your happiness. Very few desire to listen to Me and take seriously My words and invitation to love. Your way IS NOT the way to your happiness. My Way IS for you and IS for your happiness. Peace. AD DEUM.

Lesson # 14
In private chapel at home
August 1, 1995

THE NEW DAWN OF MY LIGHT

My dear little one, the dawn brings on a new day, a new day filled with My love, goodness, tenderness and gentleness. The dawn is the break from the darkness of the night when the light rises and shines through to brighten the pathway of love and the horizon of freshness, hopes and wonders. There is no more fear of the dark and uncertainty of the future. The dawn brings hope for the tomorrow of My love. The dawn enlightens and unfolds My love today. It is good, and those who persevere await the moment in hope and confidence. They know the night will end and that with time the dawn will emerge and the light will brighten the sky.

I speak these words so that My people will know that perseverance in hope will bring on the new day of goodness. Good will always prevail and love will always be victorious for all who pray, hope and work for tomorrow. Peace in your duties and faithfulness to your responsibilities will ensure victory in My love. There will always be challenges but none too difficult nor My yoke too heavy to carry. The harvest is many but the laborers are few. Those who are close to the reign of God and the kingdom of Goodness work diligently interiorly and exteriorly challenging themselves to grow in My love and mercy, and to be Me. They know the darkness of the night will pass and they hope in perseverance for the dawn of My light. Change takes time. Gentleness is what is needed to meet the challenges of the new dawn. They know it is most necessary to meet all challenges with love and to move ahead valiantly and with courage. They know they will meet failure and vices of their flesh along their journey. But they also know that love is the sword which slays these failings and that gentleness of self will assuredly make them victorious in My love. And when the new dawn of My light approaches, it will find them waiting with patience, confidence and hope, having persevered through the night. I will take these My few laborers and give to them My crown of glory; and they shall help all those who are lost on the way, those who started on the path but became distracted from persevering and stranded themselves in the cloud of confusion. They will be found by my laborers and brought back once again to the pathway of love and will be encouraged to continue on in hope, meeting with courage all obstacles and challenges. With love, gentleness and perseverance they also will rise above them. Look to the dawn, which is sure to rise, the dawn of hope for all who persevere and endure. Peace, little one. Peace to all My people. AD DEUM.

Lesson #15
In private chapel at home
August 4, 1995

LOVE AS I LOVED, DIE AS I DIED

My dear little one, you cannot worry about what will happen tomorrow. You need not focus on anything but what you are to do today or you will experience anxiety and uncertainty. It is good to plan, but do not be consumed with making sure that your plans are fulfilled. Allow God's will to unfold in the midst of your plans. Maintain peace of heart and serenity. You cannot make something happen just as you cannot make someone love you. I cannot make My people love Me. It is their free will that I have given to them as a gift. No matter how much you try to impress people or prove to them you have changed from your old ways, and no matter how kind you are to them, giving gifts of love, you cannot gain their acceptance or trust. They have free will to choose what and who they desire to love and accept. That is why I have told you to focus on Me your Lord, nothing more, nothing else, nothing less. You will gain peace and serenity of heart in My love. You will always have My acceptance and My love. You need not prove to Me that you have changed, for I have given you the grace to change. You need not try to impress Me. My love is unconditional, and it is I who bear gifts of love for My people.

People can be very cruel. When they choose their way above God's Way, when they decide not to walk the path of love I have walked before them, they lose sight of truth and reality. They become blinded by the consuming desire to fulfill their quest, and in the process they become very cruel in nature and behavior. What they define as freedom and the reign of freedom is not the stepping stone to unconditional love, but that of control and manipulation. That is why I continually invite all people to return to God, to love unconditionally and to be merciful. Many of My little ones become targets of pain from the belittling comments and cruel words of others. They try to give of themselves unconditionally in love and in the process are lashed out at in return for their efforts. These My little ones many times feel abandoned by God, but it is not so. As my little ones turn to Me and refocus once again on My love, they are strengthened and become the pillars of My unconditional love. Step by step they become victorious in the eyes of God and merit the crown of glory.

Why must it be so? Because, little one, all who love as I love must die as I died. It was My people who made their fate by their verdict they passed on Me. They made their own fate by their judgment on Me. Now all who live as I live and desire to share in My glory must die as I died, in love and in humility. Remember, I was victorious in death, and in love of My people I died in order that all might live and share in My reign. I would do it again, for My love for My people surpasses all love. Those who desire to follow this love must walk the walk, carry their cross and be crucified in My crucifiable love and mercy. Peace this day, little one, as the mysticism of My love unfolds in all its wonders. AD DEUM.

Lesson #16
In Assisi
September 9, 1995

LITTLE CHILDREN OF HOPE

My dear little one, I speak to many of My people awaiting a response of love. I desire for all people to unite and to love and to live in harmony, yet the forces of evil cause division when there is no response in faithfulness to My Word. My love alone sustains all people. Without My love nothing could exist. My love speaks to all people, but not all have chosen the Way. So I speak to many of My people in different forms, and I await a response in simplicity and faithfulness. Today in this age there is much chaos and confusion because of great division. The intellect makes a conscious effort to excel in power and control. I am looking for those who desire to be little children and for those who will guard My Word through faithfulness, love in action, and complete satisfaction in surrendering to Divine Providence. Very few of My people have chosen this route, yet My Mother, your Mother of the living, chose this simple little Way and Her power exceeds that of all creatures. Her consciousness did not gain Her power through Her intellect, but Her unconscious union with the Spirit in love and faithfulness gained Her the title of Queenship over mankind. Her feminine simplicity, Her "fiat," and Her fidelity to God were the bonds of unity and bridge of life for all of mankind. In Her resided the purity of all life, and through Her "fiat" came forth salvation for all mankind.

Why do I seek those who are little children in simpleness and yet of little influence? Because they listen and are totally dependent on Me. In their dependency stems a solid mature spiritual character, one different and unique from each other and all people. They march valiantly in the wisdom of silence of the heart, a silence where love dwells and peace resides. The voice of their prayers slays the dragons of evil and those who desire violence and destruction. I love My little ones and invite all to follow the way of littleness as that of My Mother, so secure in Her fidelity to follow God at all costs without consolation or promises. I desire children of hope, those who will continue to fight the battle through prayer and little ways regardless of the current events of the world. They have hope always, for My little ones have Me. I do not desire My children to pray and then give up their prayers because they do not see the results they desire. The battle is in the heavens against evil, and much prayer, fidelity to faithfulness, and simplicity in surrendering to God are the powerful tools of victory. Unity is what is needed. Peace is needed. All people need to join in peace and unity. But evil forces chase away those who are weak in prayer. The time of victory is for God alone to choose. When many of My little children see continual division and brokenness, they begin to doubt whether their prayers are to any avail. Consequently, they stop praying because of their lack of faith and trust in My Word. I do not desire those to surrender prayer because they have not seen the results they desire. Never surrender prayer! Surrender your heart in love for My Word to Me and pray, pray, pray! The battle will be won through prayer and unity. Be persistent hope-filled children. Have perseverance and hope in your God of love. Do not settle for less. Do not allow your consciousness to convince you to stop praying. Master all feelings through endurance and perseverance. Pray, pray, pray! Remain faithful and hope in My love! Peace, little one. My peace I give to My people. AD DEUM.

Lesson #17
In Laverna, Italy (site where St. Francis received the stigmata)
September 10, 1995

THE SILENCE OF THE HEART

My little one, in today's world people do not take the time to reflect on God's goodness in silence. They are busy seeking enticements of the world, and speech is often what becomes their companion over silence. Yet when My people are in need , they briefly come to Me and are quick to ask for graces on behalf of their needs without taking the time for contemplation and prayer in gratitude. My people speak too much and do not listen with their hearts. How I desire to fill My people with fond joy in their hearts through silence. Those who desire silence and prayer many times struggle because of the many people who violate their silence with disrespect and lack of compassion. I desire My people to take the time to reflect in silence on My love and My will for them. If My people are too busy to take time to reflect on My love, how can they discern what My will is for them? It is through prayer and contemplation that peace resides in the heart. In peace can you discern the Way of God. Prayer and contemplation allow you to be at peace with yourself, no matter what distractions or confusion surround you.

My people take little time for silent prayer and many do not take any time for silent meditation. Then when confusion and chaos strike, they are not able to find peace within. Consequently, only few of My people are able to know the truth and follow My Way.

Most importantly, I want to speak to My people and fill them with all they desire: the freedom, the peace, the joy, wisdom and happiness of the heart; but they deny themselves and Me by not adhering to My request to pray within the silence of the heart. Confusion and chaos will only continue if no one believes in My Word to reflect in prayer on My will and My love. How can you live My Word if you do not reflect on it? How can you understand the meaning of My Word and discern it as it pertains to your life and My will for you if you do not respect My gift of silence? There is a time for speech and a time for silence. I tell you few of My people know the time for silence. When you are able to reflect in silence, you will see there are more speakable words in your heart than those found on your lips.

It is good, little one, that you have come back to My place where I spoke first to you about silence. Now you see there are many people who seek in pilgrimage their needs from Me and who fail to see that one of the greatest gifts of My merciful love is silence of the heart in order that their needs would be fulfilled. I have so many graces to give; and yet, there are so few who truly desire them. They ask, ask and ask, but do not allow Me to give because My gift to them they choose not to receive. It is not in the format they expect and so they block the truth and light in answer to their request. Pray for their needs. I love My people. I desire to unite with them more intimately; and yet, I wait for them. I will wait and continue to wait for them because of My great love for them. Simplicity of life and My will for you reside in the silence of

25

your heart! Seek me there and you shall find Me and your joy. Peace to you, little one. My blessings and love. AD DEUM.

Lesson #18
In Assisi
September 11, 1995

MY LITTLE CHILDREN, MY SAINTS

My dear little one, I love My people. I love to be with them. I am the innocent, gentle Son of Man who was betrayed and condemned to death. I in My innocense carried sorrow in My heart for all the world. The wickedness of the world stood before Me and condemned Me. Yet the world thought it was I who stood in sentence before them. My acceptance of their sentence was so that they would not die. I accepted the sentence of death for them, for all people, that the body might die by the sword but the soul could live forever for all those who believed in Love. The foolish man is one who does not believe in God. For those who do not believe God exists will betray their very selves, and their own wickedness will condemn them. But for those who believe in My salvation through My victory in death will joyously celebrate and be with their gentle God. The wicked and righteous shall be slayed by their very own sword, but the innocent and meek of heart shall live for all eternity. I shall stand by My people always even though many, one by one, have chosen and are choosing to walk away from Me. Those who desire to remain with Me, I in My infinite wisdom chastise now in order that they will reign with Me and share in My glory. I desire to teach them now and encourage them to be "little" children, little in all ways: actions, thoughts, deeds and speech; little through simplicity and humility of heart.

Do not mistake littleness with lack of power. Littleness is detachment from possessions and is purity of heart. It is simpleness and the wisdom to avoid the influence of wickedness. Littleness is not associated with the lack of wealth, prestige or success. Those who are little joyfully surrender all their attachments to this world and persevere with endurance. It does not bother them not to have any attachments because they are dependent on Me and are attached to Me. Initially the surrender of their possessions may involve disheartening feelings along with temptations for the sweet enticements of the world; but as My little ones accept and renew daily their invitation to allow Me to love them, they master their feelings and find that even their feelings are attachments and obstacles to purity and humility of heart. They, with time and perseverance, become little children, pure and joyfully free, yet powerful and full of My heavenly treasures.

O' little one, how I invite all people to share in My great glory as My saints. My saints were little in the world, yet powerful because they chose to master their feelings by surrendering any possession or attachments to the world which might have prevented them from listening to My will and responding. The less the world gave to them, the more they received from Me. I invite all My people to be My little children, My saints. I love all and call all to My Heart. I wait to see who will answer and respond to My call from heaven above, for those who respond will be My little children, My saints. Bless you, little one, and continue to pray for all people in the world and for peace and unity. AD DEUM.

Lesson # 19
In Assisi
September 12, 1995

THE PATH TO MY FATHER

My dear little one, God the Father is loving and wise. Many of My people have a wrong image of My Father. That is because you cannot go to the Father except through Me. All who know Me know the Father. Few people truly know My Father. I take each person to the Father when it is the proper time. The Father desires to have an intimate relationship with all people, but in order to love the Father it is necessary to love Me. In order to love Me it is necessary to love life, to love all people, and to walk the path of My Word, Truth, and Light. The path I walked was designed by My Father. To know Him is to know His path and to cherish it. I am the Path to

My Father. I am the Truth and the Light for the world. Those who receive Me receive Him Who sent Me.

Wisdom comes through loving and simplicity. Wisdom penetrates the heart in the silence of prayer. Those who fear God in all humility have received the first grace of wisdom, for God is all-powerful and all-knowing. Those who are reverent are also wise. Wisdom leads to knowledge of His love and the comfort of His intimate protection. Those who do not believe God exists have no fear of Him. This is their foolishness being exemplified through their lack of knowledge. True knowledge in God sustains a "holy" fear of Him because what is realized is the little amount of knowledge one has compared to Him. Those who do not believe God exists believe they are all-knowing and righteous. They become calloused and arrogant instead of humble and meek. They become weak, yet they think they have gained power.

The less you realize you know, the more you gain from My heavenly Father; for in your humility you allow Him to grace you with the knowledge of His love. To know Him is to love Him. Wisdom gains you knowledge. To know Him is to be wise. To be wise is to love. To love is to be One with Me. To be One with Me is to be One with My Father, for We are One. My Father has so much to give. His love is endless. He is tender and kind and comforts all in their pain. Yet few seek Him and few desire to have a truly personal relationship with Him because they keep their distance from Me. There is nothing that God will not forgive in His merciful love when a repentant heart asks for His mercy and forgives himself. Those who seek God's mercy are humble and they enter the gateway to wisdom and holiness. To seek His mercy is to have a "holy" fear. I lead all to the Father and I show mercy when approached with a sincere heart. Many are so distant and many choose not to know Him. There are many who are afraid to come to Me even after I have told them of My mercy and My Father's love. My Father has so much to give to His little children who desire to be dependent on Him and trust Him. I invite all to come to Me so I can take all to My Father.

Pray, little one, for all people to desire the truth and love of God the Father. Their image of the Father will change when they gain wisdom and come to know Him. Pray, little one, pray. For My

Father is Good and gives all that is good. He gives life. He has given the greatest Gift of Me to all. Peace this day. AD DEUM.

Lesson #20
In Assisi
September 13, 1995

THE GIFTS OF PRUDENCE
AND DISCERNMENT

My little one, praise be to God the Father, tender, kind and all-giving. As I continue to teach My people, I desire for them to learn to utilize prudence and the gift of discernment. It is most necessary to always test the spirit of humanness against that which is Divine. All that is from God will bear good fruit and will come to pass in God's time. Patience and endurance are necessary in order to remove the human ways from being obstacles to that which is Divine. The fragrance* that bears good fruit carefully and quietly unfolds in God's time. Many times God's time seems slow to mankind. But according to God's standard, time is eternity and all that is good is molded and unfolds with the gentle stroke of the Father's Hand. (* Good wine must ferment for many years to receive the savoring, delicate taste to the lips.)

This is not to say that one who is good shall not suffer or be afflicted with temptations. In suffering is gained patience. If you are ostracized, it does not mean you are bearing bad fruit. Remember the false prophets were highly praised by many people. No, when you are scorned and troubled, mocked, ridiculed and slandered, the fruit you bear is fermenting from bitterness to savoring sweetness. Therefore, be at peace when God allows you to be chastised and pressed through the mill of sweet graces. Utilize prudence in all you do and say, and you shall see with the eyes of God His loving Hand guiding each situation in your life. Prudence teaches you to wait, pray, and not to act on emotion but out of love. Discernment teaches you counsel and allows you to weigh what is good and bad, and what you must do to follow Me. Avoid evil with silence and love. Do not partake in evil by fighting back. Genuinely love and focus on Me and your journey. Discernment teaches you to focus. All you do must center around Me. If it does not, then discernment will tell you that it is not the way for you. Discernment prevents you from straying if you utilize prudence and the counsel of its gifts.

I love all My people, yet there is much evil today. The battle in the heavens continues. Spirits of evil are trying to confuse and distract My beloved ones. All people can be subject unless they pray fervently, center on Me, and utilize prudence and discernment. Test all spirits. Desire only that which is Divine. Remain humble, simple and meek of heart. Any confusion will disipate with patient endurance and fervent prayer. You will not stray nor will any forces of evil ever conquer you if you do as I have said. I am your Lord God, here to protect and save all My little ones, all those who desire to be with Me, to walk with Me, to live in Me, to **be** Me. Bless you, little one. Pray for peace in the world. Pray for all My people. Pray for prudence and discernment and that all may be free and rejoice in My love. AD DEUM.

Lesson #21
In private chapel at home
October 4, 1995

THE GIFTS OF PIETY AND CONFIDENCE

My dear little one, when My people come to Me and love surpasses all measures, they are bound to Me in the gift of piety. They receive confidence in My love and in My care for them. Piety is having knowledge of God, but the gift allows you to perform your obligations to others out of the affection you bear for them in your heart. It is not out of justice or a duty but a measure of love, a love which passes all limits. You join a fraternity with your brethren and your soul overflows with a love you bear for them. Confidence fills you when you allow yourself to belong to Me, to trust in Me like a little child trusts a parent. This littleness allows you to rise spiritually to great levels of achievement in My love. You attain the perfection of My love. When someone comes to you for help, reflect on your motives. If you give to him out of obligation or duty, you limit the gift you can receive. Give out of the great affection of your heart and you will master this gift of piety. Love has no measures or standards. You can join in human fraternity through a genuine love and affection for each soul. To be pious is to put total confidence in Me. It is to surrender unconditionally and entrust everything to Me. It is to embrace Me with a Divine filiation. This type of unlimited confidence allows sin to be expiated. Your life becomes a reflection of Mine, both in pain and consolations. Love separates you from everything. It separates you from social position, wealth and anxiety. It liberates you in My freedom; yet, it will also strip your soul of its material cover, giving you the great consolation of freedom. Do not look to justice but to mercy. Bear a great affection for your brethren of love. I love all My people and desire them to see the many masks which shield their souls from the truth. Liberate in total freedom through love of Me and confidence in Me. Give to one another out of love not out of duty. Do not seek justice, seek mercy. Love has no measures.

Blessings on My beloved people. Peace to all. Pray for all in love for them and share your gifts by utilizing the many graces you have received in order that you will attain more. Unfathomable graces of love and mercy are yours. AD DEUM.

Lesson # 22
In private chapel at home
October 5, 1995

MY BLESSING OF PEACE

My dear little one, My blessing of peace is for all who desire it. My blessing, however, encompasses both love and pain; for both good and evil exist. If only love existed, joy would sustain the world; but there also exists evil, and much pain and sorrow have surfaced. My peace is for all who experience love, joy and pain or sorrow. My peace can exist in all situations and circumstances. My peace is unending, and it is abiding in the grace of My love. Many of My beloved people are suffering on the cross, yet they know the cross is their sanctification, which glorifies the Father; and therefore, they accept the will of God and possess great peace. Much of the world today does not desire sanctification through the means of My cross. Many people (a very great percentage currently in your world) desire to reach sanctification through their own designs. They desire to travel a path marked with fallacies and superficial piety which lead only to further degradation, corruption and chaos. No longer do My people desire to follow My Word. Instead they desire to revise My Word and then follow it. In revising the Word, they live a word made by humankind. My people no longer are open for Me to be their God. Their hearts have grown cold, and they have grown stubborn in their ways.

I, your Lord God Who Am, desire to free all from captivity. I would free them from their enemies. I would fill them with the finest gifts. But they desire not to heed My voice, so I have left them to their own designs in their stubborness. They desire to be free from the cross, and they desire a foreign god. These are **My** people who no longer desire Me to be their God. I Am Who Am! I Am the Lord God. I made the Word. I Am the Word. The Word cannot change, for I Am. There can be no other god, for I Am. But I will leave My people to their designs, and then the time will come when all will know the truth. My love and unfathomable mercy will never cease. The only boundary will be what My people place before Me and their own selves. I will never change, and I will continue to wait for all to come to Me. All are invited. My doors will remain open for all until the designated time when My Father closes them after He releases His angels to unseal the scrolls of judgment for the World. Now I continue to wait and accept even the least prayer for mercy. I continue to take the few people of the world whose prayer is to remain faithful to Me. I take their prayer and place it in My Most Sacred Heart. I store their prayers and will release My mercy because of their faithfulness.

God is infinite, little one, and My people have made mockery of My truth. Many have made mockery of My beloved Vicar on earth and have systemized and categorized moral values. My Heart is saddened by their denial of the truth, but I will not invade their domineering force because of their free will and because I am not invited to free them. I am meek, humble and gentle of heart. I love all people; and yet, all may walk away from Me and I will still love them. Judgment will come at the time My Father wills. Only then will they know the opportunity of life they have forfeited by denying the Word and revising it to meet their own designs. Pray for all people, for unity and fidelity to God. It only takes a few to change the world, a few people who are committed and devoted to the Truth at all costs. I bless you, little one, as I bless all My people. My blessing rests on all who receive it unconditionally and gratefully. Peace. AD DEUM.

Lesson #23
In private chapel at home
October 6, 1995

THE BREADTH AND DEPTH OF MY LOVE

My dear little one, My words I give to My people are in hope that they will realize the breadth and depth of My love for them. Many of My people feel unworthy because they are weak in virtue and imperfect in love. My life was for them and My love is theirs. Evil influence and weaknesses of the flesh continually crash as waves on the soul to distract and persuade it that I am a vengeful God. The fact and truth is that I am merciful, forgiving, compassionate and understanding. The opportunity is there for My beloved ones to utilize. This opportunity is within their reach and it entails a humbling of the inner self, accepting their weaknesses and turning to Me in confidence and trust for strength and mercy. The soul is revived and the Breath of Life gains for them the strength to persevere. All my people are special to Me. Each soul was created to love and to give God great glory. In giving God glory they in turn are sanctified and purified so that they may receive the same glory. I do not desire My loved ones to be downtroddened, troubled or discouraged; for I am a God of hope. I do not desire My loved ones to feel that they will not be able to possess eternal life and therefore become more distant from My love. These temptations only have one agenda, and that is to weaken them further and widen the gap between the truth of My love for them and their position.

Come, all My loved ones. I will not reject you. Draw near to My most merciful Sacred Heart. I desire to fill you with strength and hope and to encourage you to open your hearts to an intimate relationship. When you recognize your sinfulness and weakness but turn to Me humbly for mercy, I bless you, teach you and give you the power to rise to the limits of compassion and love for self. This gives God great glory when the soul recognizes that alone it merits nothing, but through God merits eternal life. For in Him all power is gained. This littleness is a dependency of trust and it surrenders unconditionally at all times and in all circumstances and situations to God's will. Simpleness of life and satisfaction in God's designs lend to the achievement of great heights in your sanctification. I did not give My life in vain. I gave my life for all people. I desire all to know that I am here and I am not distant. But I am waiting for My beloved people to allow Me to be Who I Am, for I cannot change to meet their needs or change to their liking. I am a God of love, and all My works can only end in love. When I begin to change situations of great need in peoples' lives, it seems at first the situation becomes more hopeless. That is because the circumstance initially commenced and was controlled at a human level. I, in turn, must weed out the bitter fruit so that all will blossom with the sweetness of honey. However, many of My people prevent Me at that point to continue to prune the garden. They pull the reigns of control, and out of fear they take back what they initially gave to Me. They do not trust Me. Instead, I desire them to remove themselves even further and to trust that My mercy will prevail and that ultimately great works of goodness will surface.

Tell My people, little one, that I am a God of trust and that I can be trusted with the most hopeless situations, only to reap the most promising victories. I bless and love all My people. Trust Me. Do not feel ashamed, unworthy or hopeless. I will save you and protect you if you will allow Me. The risk is in your hands. The decision is yours, for I have given you free will. I await to assist you at your call. Come, draw near. I am your Jesus of Mercy. Peace. AD DEUM.

Lesson #24
In St. Maria Goretti Church, Scottsdale, Arizona
October 13, 1995

YOUR JOURNEY OF LIFE

My little one, the daily journey of life entails a variety of emotional valleys and hills, valleys of sorrow and hills of joy. I your Jesus of Mercy walk with My people on their journey, when invited. Even though the tide changes and ways of life change for many people, I remain the same, for I am God. My Word remains the same, for I am the Word. I am Love, and I can only love. I love all My people. Even though all the world may turn against you and forget you, I will always love you and never forget you. The measure of love that I have for all My people is greater than the sands of the earth. No small deed of mercy, love, charity or compassion goes unnoticed. All are accounted for in My Kingdom. Even though the flesh dies, the soul lives and is free in My love. The bones of the flesh remain on the earth, but the spirit ascends to everlasting life, connecting life on earth to life eternal. This connection is through the cross.

It is necerssary to live in this world sharing the graces which are Divine with all people, helping all to know My love. This can be accomplished by being Love itself. You may not feel that you belong to this world, but you must live in it. Utilize the opportunity to love, and be humble and meek of heart. Pray unceasingly in mind and spirit. There are many of My beloved ones who do not know Me and are thirsty for My love. Many are confused, downtroddened, angry, bewildered and lonely. Be Love for them. **Be Me..** Bring My people to Me through unconditional love, deeds and prayer. There are many who know Me, yet are so afraid to take a risk for Me. They are quite comfortable in the way they live and in their knowledge of Me. Yet, they are not willing to be challenged by Me, nor do they desire to know Me more intimately for fear of what I might ask of them once illumination of their minds and souls commences. They keep a distance from Me. Bring these My people to Me through your example of living and of trust in Me. Let your life show them the freeedom and joy affiliated with the surrender of affection toward the passions and material possessions of the world. Your life must be an example of prayer, joy and service. It must be free of fear, anxiety and attachments of all sorts. There are many of My beloved ones who refuse to know Me. They do not desire Me. They have no interest in anything Divine. Bring these My people to Me through prayer. Unite them unceasingly to Me in the silence of your heart and live in My hope for their future. The time will come when all actions will be accounted for in the heavens. Every person will be responsible for his or her actions. It is I who desire all to be free and happy and to live in love of the truth. Speak up for the truth of My Word; yet speak lovingly and allow your actions to be the living testimony of your freedom in My love.

I bless you, little one of love and mercy, as I bless all My people in the world. Pray, pray, pray unceasingly and live My love for all. Peace in My love and fortitude in My truth! AD DEUM.

Lesson #25
In private chapel at home
October 25, 1995

LOVE AS I LOVE,
SEE THROUGH MY EYES

My dear child, listen to My words of mercy for My beloved people. See how through My patience I show My people how much I love them. I am a gentle God, loving all people. I am here for all people, not only a select few. All are special to Me for all were created in My likeness. It is My people who have the choice to belong to Me. I will never reject them. My beloved ones feel inferior and are afraid they are not counted among the chosen. They wonder why certain things happen to them and not to others. They place restrictions, contingencies and stipulations on themselves, and therefore block My love. They, in essence, build a wall of judgmental emotions against themselves, not permitting Me to love them. For this reason they end up rejecting My love and My graces which I desire to bestow on them. I want all My beloved to know the depth and breadth of My love for them.

Life is full of wonders, and what you do with each opportunity of each day allows you to be co-redeemers in My love. My people are filled with questions which occupy their minds, questions about themselves. I desire them to rest in My love by putting aside their frustrations and desires for self gain and to focus on loving others through My eyes. **Love as I love.** Do not be concerned on how you could do better serving others. Place the emphasis of your focus not on yourself but on loving others. Do the best you can do and be pleased that My grace has carried you through a given day. We together are joined in love. Do not become distracted with the frustrations and the enticements of the world. Your cross is your redemption; and the closer you desire to be to Me, the more you desire to **be Me**, the many more crosses you will be issued under the heavens, for true love and humility are brought to perfection through the cross. Do not attempt to analyze why some people seem to have heavier or fewer crosses in their lives. Everyone who desires eternal life and to share the Beatific Vision of the Holy Trinity has a cross. Only I know the incentives of each person's heart, and only I know what each person needs for salvation.

Pray for others. Intercede for them with your love, service and prayers. Join together as a unit of one body, one love. Do not weigh your cross against another person's. Keep your head under the yoke. Do not allow the passion of curiosity let your eyes look at what others are doing. Your eyes need to be focused on your own duties of love for the day. Be careful and notice how often in a given day you may be filled with judgmental opinions and emotions. Realize how often you are quick to form a verdict on someone's actions, words or general behavior, and thus feel that you are self-righteous. Put a stop to active, useless thoughts which can preoccupy your mind by replacing them with thoughts of love and affirmative, positive thoughts of the person. **See through My eyes** each person's goodness, and be merciful. Focus on My love and mercy and on how I love each person and am merciful not only toward the greatest sins but also the slightest imperfections and failings.

You can be merciful. You can be loving. You can **be Me,** for you were created in My goodness. It takes time to utilize and put into practice My words, as it takes time for an athlete to train and rise to a level of perfection in fitness. If you do not start , how will you reach the finish line? Begin now and be patient with yourself. As I have said to you in the beginning of this lesson, 'See how through patience I show My people how much I love them', through your patience show each other how much you love one another. Begin with yourself. Be patient with yourself as I guide you and show you how much you love yourself, so you will be able to show others how much you love them. Mercy is the key to loving. Take the step to mercy and cross the bridge of love. Peace, little one, to you and all My loved ones. My peace I give to you. AD DEUM.

Lesson #26
In private chapel at home
October 27, 1995

MY HANDS OF LOVE, SAFETY, AND PRO-TECTION

My dear little one, I am a God for all people. I created all which is in existence. I love all people for I created all people. There is nothing I cannot do or accomplish. I Am Who Am. I want all My people to know how tender, kind and loving I am. I do not want My people to be afraid of Me. The way to follow Me is to live My Word in simplicity. When you are confused, call on Me. Follow My Way in simplicity and remain patient. My saints were tempted and confused, and they met with many desolations, but they practiced patience for they knew I would come to their aid. Much unfolds for your sanctification and growth in humility. I will come in due time to give the consolation needed. Be at peace and do not lose focus on your Jesus.

Confidence in My love and trust in My assistance to help you are key elements. You hold the power in your own heart to unfold and control outcomes to many issues. The power is in the level of confidence you have in Me. The more confident and trusting you are of Me, the more pleasure you will take in maintaining peace of heart and the more freedom you will experience because of your security in My love. You will not be worried or concerned as to the future, but you will be more surrendered and detached. Power rests in your heart through confidence because you will know that I will ensure that all will go as God wills and everything will be for your happiness. When you place your confidence in Me, you never have to worry about your future. Every moment of your life is in My hands, in **My hands of love, safety and protection.** As you are subjected to trials and tribulations, confidence in Me will allow you to surrender and accept all which is sent to you with patience and meekness of heart. You never have to fear because in the end I will rescue you. This does not mean that you will be free in your life from all trials, humiliations, mortifications or desolations, for all come from heaven to prepare you for the glory of My Father's Kingdom. It does mean that utilizing the gift of confidence and trust in My Divine love and mercy will free you, protect your soul, and gain you sanctification. It takes many opportunities to practice humility and patience before perfection reaches sainthood. It is how you prepare to reach the finish line.

Always strive to be loving and master all trials and tribulations through trust and confidence. Even if you initially fail, you have not failed. Each time you have gained wisdom and have practiced the virtues of humility and patience. Each time you become more like Me until you are Me in Divine love and mercy. Never lose sight of the fact that I am always with you and that I am your God, a God for all people for I created all things in existence and all people. I am a loving God. I love all My people. Nothing unfolds unless it is allowed by My Father. Therefore, confidence in Him will secure your safety and position in His Kingdom. Trust that what unfolds in your life is to release you from the chains of this world and to gain for you true freedom and joy. There is so much you cannot see around you which inhibits your growth. My Father sees and knows what will truly make you happy. Trust in God! Trust in your Jesus of Mercy! **TRUST! TRUST! TRUST!** Do not say "yes" and then try to take back your "yes". Make your "yes" a **"YES"** and **TRUST!** Be patient. Be filled with hope and anticipation of the freedom and joy to come. Peace, little one, to you and My beloved ones, My people. Peace. AD DEUM.

Lesson #27
In private chapel at home
October 30, 1995

YOUR OWN LACK OF LOVE

My little one, I want My people to know that it is contradictory to say that you love and are merciful and then to turn around and blame others for their lack of response to their needs. You cannot say you live My Word and then turn around and judge, be indifferent, be complacent, or treat others as aliens because they do not share your belief or because you feel they are not living as children of the Father and disciples of the Son. I want My people to know that it is most important during this time that they be very careful in how they perceive others in thought, word, and deeds. Be careful how you see yourself. Do not be self-righteous and see yourself as favored, yet others as confused, lost, or in need of pity. I will not enter into the already established forum of many groups and organizations where I need to justify My Being, My Presence, My words or that of My Mother's.

What is needed is unconditional love and acceptance for all people. I am your Jesus of Mercy. I am God. Those who wish to believe My words may be at peace, and those who wish to scrutinize and scandalize My words by looking at the messenger instead of the message may also do so. But I tell you, no one is superior, self-righteous, favored, or in a more grace-filled position who cannot love unconditionally. How can you say you love Me with all your heart and desire to be Me and even study My Way and My Word, then turn around and criticize and condemn with a sense of authority? The more you humble yourself and become meek of heart will you gain authority on that which is Divine. My message of love and mercy may seem to be too simple of a task and without full flavor for many people. If this is so, why is it that so few people are responding at all levels to My words and requests? My people are filled with human anger and they fight evil with evil. They are filled with hate. Yet My people also feel they are chosen, that they will gain the Kingdom, and that they are justified in blaming others. What is needed is love at all levels for all My people regardless of title, position or authority, even in My Church. Love is what is needed. Mercy!

It is dangerous to blame others for war. It is dangerous to blame others for lack of resources. It is dangerous to blame others for lack of health. First, you must look to yourself and see **your own lack of love.** It is love which saves. It is the lack of love of which you yourself are guilty that has led to wars, crime, lack of resources, hunger and pain. LOVE! LOVE! LOVE! Many are caught up in My Mother's loving words of hope and encouragement. They say they live Her messages, yet they turn around and criticize, judge, or keep their distance from those they feel are not living as God's children. Those types of actions are not loving. Those actions are not merciful. Those actions do not yield a meek or humble heart. MY WORDS ARE TO BE LOVING AND MERCIFUL TO ALL PEOPLE. MY WORDS ARE TO BE MEEK AND HUMBLE OF HEART. MY WORDS ARE FOR ALL PEOPLE OF ALL RACES OF ALL NATIONS. If you choose to follow Me and My Word, then you will live My Word and love as I love. Regardless of the messenger, regardless of the place, regardless of your own personal opinion, you will love unconditionally and humble yourself to be like Me if you are truly My servant. Better now to search your motives than to find out later that you were filled with bloated pride.

It is because I love My people and desire them to be free that I reveal My words of truth. Those who feel uncomfortable reading My words or are quick to pass judgment on the authenticity of My words should perhaps reflect on them more deeply, for they are the ones held captive and slave to pride. It reflects their ways and their actions. It is likened to the high priest who comes before Me thanking Me that he is righteous and not like the rest of the sinners and the beggar who beats his breast pleading for God's mercy because He is a sinner. Who do you think will gain the Kingdom? Beware of your spiritual pride. Turn now away from your sinful mannerisms, and LOVE. Love yourself, love others, and love to be humble. I bless you and love you. I give to you My peace and I hope you will decide for LOVE. It is your choice. Peace. AD DEUM.

Lesson #28
In private chapel at home
November 2, 1995

THE CRY OF MY PEOPLE

My dear little one, I hear the cry of My people. I hear their plea. All is answered through My most merciful Heart. The sorrowful shall be comforted. I will not allow My people to be alone. There already has been great devastation in the world where many of My people have wailed in agony for My mercy. I come to the rescue of each soul even though agony has resulted through human hands and the unwillingness to love or be merciful. Evil's reign of power is close to an end, and there shall be no more tears of sorrow but tears of joy and gladness. Every sorrow, every whimper of pain pierces My Sacred Heart only to be turned into the soul's glory in resurrection. It grieves Me that many of My people have chosen to walk the way of evil. They have chosen to be stubborn in their ways. They want, but they refuse to give. They must be right at all times and fail to accept error in humility. Pride continues to control every element of their being; and when they receive what they have sought after, it is not enough. They desire more. Since they are never satisfied, they are never at peace. Only those who bow their heads under the yoke of God can receive true wisdom through gentleness and meekness of heart.

My servants know the way of love. My servants may suffer, but their suffering is united to Mine and is redemptive. In time every man, woman and child shall know the truth of My love. They will see the truth of the world as it is and what they have missed from postponing prayer and service through love. By seeking self-gain in the world they will see what they have depleted from their souls through the loss of treasures in heaven. Evil does exist and its subtleties linger and fall prey on any soul complacent or indifferent to unconditional love and mercy. No doubt My servants will suffer interiorly and perhaps exteriorly because of the current conditions of the world which do not render love without self-gain.

No one is ever free when there exists conditions and limitations on mercy. This is not any new discovery. I have called My people to unconditional love and mercy for 2000 years. I have invited My people to live in simplicity and to pray. I have invited My people to follow the Truth of My Way. I have told My people that it takes time to change and not to wait to the last moment. My love is not a project meeting a deadline. My love is a way of life, an ongoing peace, harmony, unity, freedom and joy. My love challenges you to grow and rise to the highest levels of dignity and respect. Wounds are healed, though perhaps not without pain. Ultimately pain will cease and no wounds will exist when you walk My Way. I have tried to help My people, but many refuse My assistance and My love. Their ways are confounded in self-pride and their pain deepens. The window of opportunity has been opened to love, but now My people in desolation, despair and pain accuse Me of abandonment. I will always remain Who I Am. I am Love. I have never changed. So few listened to My words. Many are still not listening. Who is guilty of abandonment? The window of opportunity still exists. I have never left My people. Never! Each soul is precious in My love. Each soul is invited to love and will not be turned away. Each soul is also given the freedom to choose Love. Now the world is a product of humankind's decision to love. Evil could not prevail unless allowed by the soul. Power, materialism and prestige have masked the truth of dignity. Politicians debating other politicians and leaders of other countries are all seeking their own self-gain. Few seek to uphold the truths of mercy and love for freedom in the world. This lack of genuine love and service will only be manifested in the current devastations existing in the world.

My love has filtered through many souls now seeking the truth, and many souls are allowing Me to help them. As genuine love surfaces, evil will initially seem to have stronger forces, but will weaken because evil cannot exist where there is Love. Humankind will have the opportunity to control and eliminate evil through genuine love and mercy. I will be with them as I have been before. Evil would like you to believe you have no power to control or eliminate its forces in existance. But I tell you otherwise. Through love evil cannot exist. Unity, harmony and mercy are the artillery to win the battle through love. This may mean you may not be always at the forefront in the areas of prestige, power or self-righteousness. Love has no boundaries, and the first areas evil attacks are the areas of pride, self-gain, materialism, and power: the masks of falsehood and obstacles to freedom. But many of My beloved ones are gaining the knowledge of truth from asking My assistance and giving their souls unconditionally to My care, love and mercy. There is hope for the future of mankind, a hope founded in Love. For evil's reign is close to an end. I love you, little one, and all My people. Peace be with you. AD DEUM.

Lesson #29
In private chapel at home
November 9, 1995

LET ME ORCHESTRATE YOUR TIME

My little one, come to Me when you are weary and rest in My love. I will give you peace and refresh your soul with My presence. So many of My beloved people are tired and in need of great comfort and loving care. I desire all who are tired and filled with anguish to have recourse to Me. No matter how busy your schedule is daily, I can comfort you. Only ask Me to orchestrate your time, and you will be given the time to rest in My love in prayer and solitude. If you desire time with Me, I will give it to you. I am gentle and meek of heart. I will teach you how to pray. I will lead you to a conversion of heart through praying for forgiveness and purity of heart. You will love your enemies and persecutors and seek the Kingdom above all else. You will learn to pray in faith, for I will guide you. You will **knock,** and I, being the Door, will open to you the Way. Your heart will be disposed to do the will of My Father, for you will be bonded to Him in filial love. In Me you will live the perfect model of prayer through a loving adherence to the will of My Father. Remember I have mentioned to you the bond of filial love and how you, through Me, are a child of God. Pray with confidence. Pray with a persevering faith and with purity of heart. Give all your petitions in prayer to My Father in My Name. I have told you of His great love and tender kindness. This filial bond of love with the Father is a communion with Him. Nothing happens to you in life unless My Father wills it so. Trust in Divine Providence and surrender to His consoling truths. Trust in the wisdom of God. His judgment does not lack in what is advantageous for you. Even misfortunes have a useful purpose. Practice trustful surrender and have a loving recourse to God. I will teach you to conform to the will of My Father in adversity as well as in prosperity, in times of humiliation and disgrace as well as in times of honor and respect. I will lead you and be your Teacher. Though all may turn from you, I will never leave you. I will be there for you. You will have a place to rest your weary head. I am merciful and all loving. I am your Jesus of Mercy.

I want all My people to know I am here for them at their asking. I surround them with love, and I hope they will desire the counsels of truth. It is My hope that they practice filial submnission to Divine Providence. This allows them to rest in My Father's arms as a child rests in its mother's arms. Conforming the soul in love to Divine Providence allows the soul to rest in peace and gives hope to the weary. My lessons to My people have been given because of My great love for them. I am calling My people to return back to God. I desire My poeple to know I have not abandoned them. I have given them the tools of prayer and the consoling truths of My existence. I have desired them to learn, to be free, and to grow in holiness. I give My words for them to give them hope for the journey. I await their love. My Word will never perish. All who abide in the Word abide in Me and abide in Love. Those who abide in Me abide in My Father in a filial boldness. My lessons are for **all** people in the world. All are invited to live in unity, peace and love. All are invited to live in the truth of God. Peace to all, little one. My peace I give to you for all eternity. Come, you who are weary and filled with anguish. Come, rest in My love. Receive My mercy and comforting love. I am your Jesus of Mercy. AD DEUM.

Lesson #30
In private chapel at home
November 11-12, 1995, midnight

RETURN TO GOD

My dear little one, if ever I wanted to stress upon My people the importance and significance of prayer, there would be no more opportune time than the present. I am not asking My people to give Me all of their undivided attention. I am asking them to return back to God and to give even a little of their time in prayer and thanksgiving to My Father for all the wonders He gives to all people continuously and unconditionally. If all My people would pray daily even for a small amount of time, there would be peace and unity. Some of My beloved ones are praying, yet many are not. If **ALL** would pray, there would be peace through love and mercy. I desire to give to My people all good things from above. I have given My words of love and My teachings in hope that My people will return to the Way of truth. The future is contingent upon prayer. Much can be mitigated through prayer.

My Father is merciful and kind, especially to the repentant sinner. Just as Nineveh was spared, so too can the world in which you live be spared. Love and mercy are key elements and virtues of the truth. My Father is tender and kind. He seeks the humble hearts and He is a patient God. There is tremendous hope for the journey for all who desire to know and live the truth. I would like to continue to give My lessons to My people, but I have given My Word through the Scriptures, and I am still waiting for My people to live My Word. My Word is **THE** Word. It is already written. It has been available to My people for 2000 years. No new words will make any difference if My Word through Scripture is not practiced. My beloved priests, bishops, cardinals, deacons, religious, nuns, and even Christian evangelicals and ministers may have **studied** My Word, but I have invited **ALL** My people of the world to **live** My Word. There comes a time, little one, when no additional words from Me will make any difference or make a greater impact on people. Those who desire My Word have it already. For those who do not desire to know My Word, then no other words from Me will change their hearts.

Pray for all people. Pray and love all people, even those who seem to be farthest away. Do not be afraid to pray for those who are your enemies. Do not harden your hearts, but walk through clouds of anger and bitterness and meet them with love, strength and mercy on the other side. There is no need to take justice into your own hands. There is no need to take prosecution to the full extent of the law. What are needed are contrite hearts, merciful hearts, patient hearts, and hearts of compassion. Those who live My Word have hearts of love, mercy, patience and compassion. Those who do not **live** My Word have hearts of stone and live not in My world but in their own. You cannot serve two masters. Those who live by My Word of truth and love know that justice will be fulfilled at the hand of My Father. You cannot say you are a child of God, a chosen people, and then through words and actions contradict the law of love as I have given it to you. If you pray, you will know the truth, for the least contradiction to loving would cause inner division, for love and hate are not able to be mixed.

I await My people to return to Love. This does not mean that man is perfect or will not fail. If that were the case, My death for love of you would have been in vain. It means that through prayer and humility in accepting yourself in failure, you are able to grow in holiness and reach the Kindgdom through patience and the virtues dispensed from God. It does not mean that you are not to live by the law established by mankind for structure and organizational standards in society. What is needed to return to God is to live in a world by the virtues of love and dignity, not revenge, resentment, or hatred. It is so necessary, little one, that My peopele return to Me **soon,** before it becomes any more difficult to change. The longer My people delay, the colder the heart becomes, more and more like stone. But prayer, love and mercy chip away at the stony heart, and soon enough purity radiates beneath all layers.

I am here, little one, for all people. I love all people. I died for all people, and I would die again if I could because of My love for all people. Listen to the teachings of My Church. Listen to My Word and live it. Just take a few minutes to be with Me, to ponder

My love in your life. I want to call all My people to Me. Return to God, My loved ones. Please return. Change the current path towards human destruction to one of love, peace, unity and life. Live in freedom through living the truth of My Word. I shall not give any new words until My people begin to live My current words, for all is written. My Word will not change. It stands as is for I am the living Word. Those who live in Me live My Word. So many have chosen to walk away. Come, return to My love. Live My Word of truth. I love you, My beloved people. I am your Jesus of Mercy. I am Love, and I have so much to give you, more than you could ever imagine. Come, come to Me. Return back to Me. Return to God. All I can ask of you and all I can invite you to is to **RETURN TO GOD!**

AFTERWORD

Fr. Frederick M. Jelly, O.P.
Professor of Theology
Mount St. Mary's Seminary
Emmitsburg, MD

As a Dominican priest and theologian, I have found the thirty messages of Jesus in this volume to be a source of special inspiration. Our motto as the Order of Preachers in the Church (O.P.) has been "contemplare, et aliis tradere contemplata," which may be rendered into the vernacular "to contemplate, and to hand on to others the fruits of our contemplation." Throughout the lessons of this volume, Gianna Talone-Sullivan has shared with us the fruits of her own contemplative prayer as she reports the teachings of Jesus calling us to a deeper mystical union with the Father through Him, which is the necessary spiritual experience for all apostolic activity.

Although such titles as "contemplative apostle" and "apostolic contemplative" are not used in these lessons of "Jesus of Mercy," nevertheless they are very apt to summarize their constant refrain. The infused virtue of love permeates every message in this volume, the love of God and of neighbor that embraces both the prayers of the contemplative and the actions of the apostle called to be disciples of Christ. Christ himself unites in his own divine personality the eternal contemplative love of the Father in the Holy Spirit with the mission of redeeming us through the deeds and sufferings of his real human nature. Mary, the first and foremost of his disciples in the Church, united the love of the contemplative at the Annunciation with the active love of the apostle at the Visitation in sharing with others (especially John the Baptizer in Elizabeth's womb) the sanctifying presence of the Word made flesh in her own womb made fruitful by the Holy Spirit.

We are all called by our baptismal vows "to live the Word" as is so often said in these lessons of the merciful Jesus. Each in his/her own way, whether lay person, religious, or priest, is given the special graces to help make the redeeming love of the Word made flesh present to our world today. May our meditating on these lessons inspire us to do so with greater wisdom and love.

PART II

Messages from Our Lady of Emmitsburg
(St. Joseph's Roman Catholic Church
Emmitsburg, Maryland)

November 1993 - March 1996

Messages received through
Gianna Talone-Sullivan

Our Lady's Message of November 3, 1993
through Gianna Talone Sullivan

My dear little children, praise be Jesus!

My little ones, I am your Lady of Joy.

I bring you tidings of love and peace.

My little, little children, love unconditionally.

Strive always to abandon yourself unconditionally to God, so that you will be able to love unconditionally.

Do not allow self-deceit to pull you away from My Son.

Even when you think you are loving in purity as Jesus would have you love, you can fall into loving according to your standards.

Love unconditionally.

Love all.

It is very important that abandonment of yourself be a daily offering to My Son, so that you can love in purity, unconditionally, as Jesus would have you love.

It is in loving that you are united to the Triune God.

Bless you, My little ones.

Bless you in the name of Jesus.

Peace.

Thank you for responding to My call.

(Our Lady blessed everyone and prayed over everyone.
She took petitions of the heart in love tonight.)

Our Lady's Message of November 10, 1993
through Gianna Talone Sullivan

My dear little children, praise be Jesus!

My little ones, remember I have said every prayer which is from the heart is another rose which is given to My Son.

My little ones, pray with all your heart.

Do not only recite words, but sing with songs of praise, every word through your heart.

My Son wants your heart, not your words.

He wants your actions to speak your words.

My Son loves you, My little ones.

I wish for all of you to know truly how present I am to you, all of you.

My Son has gifted you to allow Me to be here with you in this special way.

That is why I ask you to take seriously My calling.

Tonight I again speak words of unity and harmony.

It is time, My little ones, that you begin to live in unity.

There are far too many people living in ways of division and unmerciful means through lack of kindness.

Please return back to God.

Pray with your heart and He will guide you how to live in unity through loving.

Please, please, please **love** one another.

How can I give you new messages if you are not living these existing ones?

I need you My little ones and I bless you in My Son's name.

Blessed be God.

Thank you for responding to My call.

(Our Lady was tearful tonight. When asked why, she said there are too many leaders and not enough servants.)

Our Lady's Message of November 17, 1993
through Gianna Talone Sullivan

My dear little children, praise be Jesus!

My little ones, I come to you as a gift from God in these times of great need, in order that you will return back to God.

I have come so frequently because little is being paid in attention to My messages.

My little ones, please heed My words.

I am calling you to great prayer and love and patience.

I desire to intercede for you to God, imploring His mercy.

My Son loves you, My little ones, and all focus should be on Him.

Allow Me to help you pray and allow Me to intercede for you.

I ask you this night for your patience.

Take the pain of patience in the trouble of your brother.

Remember, My little ones, that if you cannot be patient with your own imperfections, how can you expect others to be perfect?

Bear with patience all tribulations of yourself and others.

Focus on Jesus.

He loves you.

There is far too much expectations on men and this results in impatience, bitterness and hatred.

I love you and desire to teach you what My Son has asked Me.

I bless you My little ones and thank you for responding to My call.

Our Lady's Message of November 24, 1993
through Gianna Talone Sullivan

My dear little children, praise be Jesus!

My little ones, do you realize that because of the current condition of the world, if I were to come to you only one time, **no one** would listen to My words of plea?

But because My Son loves you so **unconditionally**, He has humbled Himself to allow Me to come to you in a very present way, to help you and ask your **unconditional** love.

As your **Mother**, I ask you to humble yourself to My Son.

Go before Him in the Blessed Sacrament, smother Him with love, in order that He will mitigate what is to come.

Do not ask Him to fulfill your personal needs.

He knows what you need for eternal happiness.

Simply love Him and praise Him, for He is your God.

He is the Son of God.

You have all become too indifferent, failing to realize who is your God.

Your mortal, human ways have caused division and scattered destructiveness because of your desire to control.

I am now pleading with you in these last days that I am permitted to be here, to love Jesus and follow His ways, outlined in the Scripture.

Is there not one of you who will love My Son without expecting consolation in return?

How can I help you if, when He tests you, you will not allow Me to be your Mediatrix of Grace?

Put aside your human desires and look to that which is Divine.

I bless you, My little ones.

I love you and I am thanking you for taking seriously this call to love.

Peace to you in the name of Jesus!

He is your God, whether you wish to acknowledge that or not.

The day will come that all will know the truth.

Peace.

(This Message is requested by Our Lady to be
read to **all**. Our Lady was **very** serious.)

Our Lady's Message of December 1, 1993
through Gianna Talone Sullivan

My dear little children, praise be Jesus!

My little ones, pray that you will receive the grace to abandon yourself unto God.

It is through abandonment that you become free and are receptive to do God's will.

My Son loves you and it is through detachment from the world and in being open to His way through obedience,that you can be at peace, to love and receive great graces.

My Son wishes to grace you with many virtues, but first the vices of the flesh must be tempered.

My Son wishes for all to receive My virtues of patience, faith, love, sweetness, wisdom, charity, humility, obedience, hope and prayer.

I love you, My little children, and ask you to pray fervently to Jesus.

Pray, be patient, pray and please love one another unconditionally.

Love as a decision and your heart will live out His love, if you abandon yourself to My Son.

Bless you, My little ones, in the name of Jesus.

Thank you for responding to My call these days I have been allowed to be here.

Our Lady's Message of December 8, 1993
through Gianna Talone Sullivan

My dear children, I am your Mother of the Immaculate Conception.

I am your Mother of Joy.

Praise be Jesus!

Praise His Holy Name.

My little ones, you are all called to a life of purity, a life free of sin, a life filled with joy, happiness and peace.

Satan would like you to dwell on your sins.

He would like you to live in shame, guilt and be unforgiving to yourselves and others.

In prayer you will realize that Jesus loves you and is calling you not to sin, shame or guilt, but to freedom, joy, purity and forgiveness.

Receive His love.

Utilize the sacrament of reconciliation and you will be like newborn babes.

Seek to be pure, My little ones.

Pray, live in His faith, and love one another unconditionally.

Jesus will grace you with purity if you desire this virtue.

I bless you, My little ones, and ask you to pray for purity so you will be free from the stain of sin and be whole and happy.

Thank you, My little ones, for responding to My call.

A call to purity.

Peace.

(Our Lady came with Baby Jesus. She was dressed in gold.)

Our Lady's Message of December 15, 1993
through Gianna Talone Sullivan

My dear little children, praise be Jesus!
My little ones, please be calm.
Rest in My Son's Sacred Heart.
If you lift your head from His yoke, you will be wounded.
Focus on Him!
Jesus is your protection, love and intimate friend.
Blessed are those who are meek and mild of heart.
Simple, yet so consumed by the flame of His Sacred Heart, you are
all called to be blest by being meek and humble of heart.
Focus on My Son.
He will temper your vices with love.
Love will filter into your soul and consume your entire being.
My little ones, know I take your petitions to My Son.
I will always take your petitions and present you as a loving mother
would.
You will never be forgotten by Jesus.
Even if all forget you, Jesus will never forget you.
You are precious in His eyes and He desires you so tremendously.
Tonight I bless you with the grace of meekness.
Thank you, My little ones.
I bless you in the name of My Son, who has allowed Me to be here
for you.
Thank you for responding to this call to meekness and humbleness
of heart.
Peace.

Our Lady's Message of December 22, 1993
through Gianna Talone Sullivan

My dear little children, praise be Jesus!
My little ones, how blest are you to know Jesus.
How blest you are that He in His infinite mercy and countenance
graces you with His Divine love.
My little children, Jesus is your Savior.

Do you not see interiorly how free you are because of the newborn babe?

Remember always, My little children, that through Him you can serve this world, all His children in need.

But without My Son, you cannot serve the world with love, even though humanly you can serve.

Only through Jesus can you love and only through His love can you truly serve those in need in this world.

I love you, My little children, and I give to you My greatest treasure, My Son, My heart.

Take this precious gift and cultivate the love He has given to you through loving one another.

Thank you, My little children, for your prayers.

Use this time of grace wisely, by always examining your actions.

Always, they should be actions of love for others, yourself and most importantly My Son.

Love Him first, above yourself and yourself for Him.

Then you can love others, and your actions will be fruitful in His love.

Bless you in the name of Emmanuel, your God who is with you.

Thank you for your response to My call. Peace.

(Our Lady prayed over everyone, blessed everyone and kissed me.)

Our Lady's Message of January 19, 1994
through Gianna Talone Sullivan

My dear little children, praise be Jesus!

My little ones, Jesus is your treasure.

Adore Him with all of your hearts.

Rest in Him, allowing Him to whisper words of love and courage while you adore Him in the most Blessed Sacrament.

How My Son has been waiting for you in the tabernacles of the world.

He loves you so much.

You are very important to Him.

Tend to Him and **rest** in Him.

My little ones, as this grace period soon will end, it is very important to focus on Jesus, love one another as a family and support each other with ways of love.

If you lose your focus from distraction, you will become confused.

I ask you to concentrate on your intimate relationship with My Son and do not deviate from your love for Him.

He will protect you and He will be with you.

Focus on Jesus as these unusual events unfold.

Pray, pray, pray to not be tested and that you will never lose sight of My Son.

Pray for peace, unity, harmony, purity and honesty.

I bless you, My little ones, in the name of Jesus.

Thank you for responding to My call.

Our Lady's Message of January 26, 1994
through Gianna Talone Sullivan

My dear little children, praise be Jesus!

My little ones, I come to you in joy, but also in sadness;
joy because God exists and He loves you.

You do not fully comprehend the depth of His love, but He does love you, each one of you.

But I come to you in sadness, because I have been allowed to come here to plead with you that your hearts would change.

I have asked that you seek intimacy with My Son and to make evident changes in your life that were not ways of love and harmony.

I have tried to teach you and guide you in the ways of My Son, pleading that you would not seek ways of power and worldly goals, but that which is Divine.

Many continue to take lightly My requests.

I wish with all My love to help you, but you, through your free will, must desire this heavenly way.

Please, My little ones, My Son has not allowed Me to come for little purpose.

Please take seriously My words.

Your eternal life depends on your heart's desire.

Where is Jesus in your life? Is He first?

Pray to those who rest in peace (the Saints), for they know the depth of My Son's love which you have not yet grasped.

Pray they intercede for you, that you may love as My Son.

Remember, My little ones, Jesus is Mercy, but if you will not accept His mercy, He will have no choice than to be a God of justice.

I bless you and love you, My little ones.

Please do not ignore My plea for love and interior change through God's grace.

Your life and your safety depends on securing eternal bliss.

Thank you for responding to My call.

Our Lady's Message of February 2, 1994
through Gianna Talone Sullivan

My dear little children, praise be Jesus!

My little ones, I bring you good news.

Jesus' love is everlasting and you can rest totally in Him.

Thanks be to God for His kindness and mercy which are **everlasting**.

I hear your plea, My dear ones.

Know that even though there are many of you who struggle, there is hope in My Son.

Do not be discouraged.

The good news is that you belong to God.

When you hope and trust in My Son, you can rest in peace with confidence that love and mercy is yours for all eternity.

Inner conflict and struggles may unveil, but know God loves you and wishes for you to rise to a level of wholeness.

Evil will be weeded out from the good.

You are all called to be pure and whole, to love.

There are many kinds of love, but I speak of a love of charity.

This love is kept for love of God and is supreme and sovereign.

You may not fully comprehend His love, but I ask you to rejoice in His love for you, because His love and mercy endures.

I present you this night to My Son with love and as your mother.

I ask you to focus on Him, love Him with all your hearts, and rejoice that His mercy endures forever.

Peace, My little ones. Thank you.

Thank you for responding to My call.

AD DEUM.

Our Lady's Message of February 9, 1994
through Gianna Talone Sullivan

My dear little children, praise be to Jesus!

My words to you are direct and simple this night.

I come before you asking you to pray that the challenges My Son presents to you for your good be fulfilled through abandonment.

Please, My little ones, seek to surrender every day and accept God's love.

Pray! Do not be distracted with your personal issues.

God knows what you need.

Surrender all to Him.

Pray that you will surrender and that His challenges of love will be fulfilled through your acceptance and abandonment.

Please do not be deceived these days, My little ones.

Satan would like you to be deceived.

I speak the truth and you will know this truth through prayer and surrendering to Divine Providence.

I love you, My little children.

God loves you.

I bless you in the name of Him who sent Me.

Please pray that you will surrender unto God and accept His Divine will, designed especially for your happiness.

Thank you for responding to My call.

Peace.

(Our Lady asked three times that we
surrender and accept this message.)

Our Lady's Message of February 16, 1994
through Gianna Talone Sullivan

My dear little children, praise be Jesus!

My little ones, during this Lenten season, know that the Lord loves you.

This season is one of love.

Give to Him your hearts in love.

It is to be a Lenten season of giving, forgiving, love and mortification.

Do not be blinded by that which My Son calls you to live.

Pray for the virtues to live as He, virtues of patience, humility, love, charity, self-mortification and meekness.

My Jesus is your Savior.

Pray that you will see Him as He is.

I bless you, My little children, and take your petitions to My Son's Sacred Heart.

I pray they will be fulfilled during this Lenten season of love.

Most importantly, My prayer for you is to look beyond to that which is Divine for your glory in Jesus through love and mortification, a special charitable love which will never fail you, but will always sustain you.

Thank you for responding to My call.

Peace.

AD DEUM.

(Our Lady prayed over everyone as She reminded us
of the ending of our grace period granted from our Lord
one-and-one-half years ago.)

Our Lady's Message of February 24, 1994
through Gianna Talone Sullivan

My dear little children, praise be Jesus!

I am your Mother of Joy, who so desires you to live in a world of peace.

But peace does not exist, because there is division.

There is division because of the conflict which exists on the moral values in the world.

My little, little children, do **not** alter your standards of following the Gospel in order to satisfy the needs of others.

Never deviate from the truth of His Word.

You cannot please men by jeopardizing your freedom and living deceitful ways of life.

The only way to freedom is by living the truth outlined by My Son.

He has given you His Word.

You cannot change His words and live dishonest lives and conceive that peace could even exist.

There is only **one way** and that way is the way of My Son in His Word of the Gospel.

He is your God. There is only one God.

I plead with you that you hold fast to His Word and not deviate from His stance on truth, or you will suffer tremendously through the hands of man.

I love you My little ones, and bless you.

I desire you to be happy and free, but you must return to God and live the truth of His Word.

Killings of all sorts, greed, abuse, selfishness, anger, malice, dishonesty, adultery and other sexual disgraces, self-induced and those of children, men and women, are vices which prevent your freedom.

Reconcile your sins and live in His truth.

Thank you for responding to My call. Ad Deum.

(Our Lady was **very serious**, yet Her words were in a loving tone. She was sorrowful with tears in Her eyes. Killings of all sorts included abortions. Sexual disgraces of men and women were those of homosexuality.)

Our Lady's Message of March 3, 1994
through Gianna Talone Sullivan

My dear little children, praise be Jesus!

My little ones, know you are children of God.

Seek to follow the ways of Christian perfection and walk away from the ways of wickedness.

God loves you.

Trust in God and follow His way.

The challenges and enticements of life result in shortcomings without the love and hope in God.

Do not turn your heart away from God.

Hope in Him.

During these times when God is unveiling His mercy, you need to be strong in the gift of His faith and be secure in His hope.

You must not sway in your decision to be a child of God, nor be ashamed to follow His truth when confronted with controversial topics of moral values.

You must hope and trust in God.

You must speak the truth of His Word.

It is your only security.

If you seek to please man while avoiding the truth of God outlined in His Word of the Gospel, then you will jeopardize your freedom and position of attaining eternal bliss at the time of your final judgement before Him.

I bless you, My little ones, in the name of Jesus.

Thank you for responding to My call.

(Our Lady gave a special blessing on priests around the entire world tonight. She asked us to pray for priests.)

Our Lady's Message of March 10, 1994
through Gianna Talone Sullivan

My dear little children, praise be Jesus!

Thank you, My little ones, for inviting Me to be with you.

Thanks be to God who has allowed Me to come in His name.

Tonight, My little ones, I have two requests:

Firstly, I ask you to unite with Me in prayer for My beloved priests, who are loyal to My Son and who suffer tremendously.

Their pain is endless because of their loyalty.

Pray for them especially during these times of uncertainty and troubles.

65

I love My priests. Join Me please in prayer.

Secondly, My little children, I must tell you not to trust in deceitful words.

If you focus on Jesus, trust in Him, abandon yourself unto Him and practice His words of truth, you will **not** be deceived, but live healthy, joyful lives.

Change is needed, not only in words, but in actions.

Give unconditionally, simply and lovingly to others without seeking reward or consolation for your efforts.

Wickedness must be replaced with ways of holiness.

If change is not accomplished, then the time will come that your sorrow will result at the hands of a wicked disposition, which will be its blame.

I bless you, My little ones.

I love you and take your petitions to My Son.

Thank you for your prayers for peace and thank you for responding to My call.

Peace. Ad Deum.

Our Lady's Message of March 17, 1994
through Gianna Talone Sullivan

My dear children, praise be Jesus!

My little ones, you continue to pray that the will of God be done in your lives.

Doing the will of God involves the following:

If you are religious, then being obedient to your superiors is doing the will of the Father.

If you are a superior, pray for discernment and use prudence and love.

If you are married, then be obedient to each other as spouses in the sacrament of marriage and teach your children to love and follow the way of truth outlined in My Son's word in the Gospel.

If you are single, live pure, holy lives consecrated to God.

Be honest and treat others with dignity.

Help the poor and elderly and the young.

And if you have been blessed with resources of wealth, intellect, management skills and graces to help His needy, then unite together and give to His less fortunate.

They suffer as representation of the humiliated Jesus.

Protect My unborn through love and unity.

Teach My youth, and unite all your resources in harmony.

Help My Son in His mission of mercy.

It is the way to peace.

Peace cannot exist if there is no change in moral values and in unity.

I continue to plead to God for His mercy and love.

There is **no time like the present** to commence these activities.

Prayer and love will restrain His hand of punishment from the lack of love.

It is the only way.

He is your God, the same God of Abraham, Isaac and Jacob.

If you implore His mercy and love, all can be mitigated, for everything is contingent on prayer.

Thank you for responding to My call.

Peace. Ad Deum.

Our Lady's Message of March 24, 1994
through Gianna Talone Sullivan

My dear little children, praise be Jesus!

I am your Mother of Joy who brings you the joy of My Son, your Jesus, your Savior.

My little ones, you are seeking God, but He is everywhere.

Everything speaks of Him to you.

Everything offers Him to you.

He surrounds you.

He walks with you and He is within you.

He is your living God.

He lives with you and yet you are trying to seek Him.

This is because you are seeking your own idea of God, even though you have Him in reality.

My little children, love God as He is.

You are straining after vain imaginations of who God is and are
not allowing Him to dwell with you.

Do you not see that all you do, all you suffer and all you envelop
daily are the mysteries under which God gives Himself to you?

Put aside your falsehoods and the sweet enticements of the world
and live in His truth.

Accept daily His living presence of love through all you encounter
and in all you do and in everything that surrounds you.

His Divine perfection of design is for you.

Live it fully to the best of your ability in His love.

Do not miss the moment because of false imaginations.

I thank His blessed name for allowing Me to be with you.

It is because of His love and Divine mercy.

Thank you for responding to My call. Ad Deum.

(Our Lady prayed over everyone, blessed everyone and
took our petitions in Her heart. Rays of white light of
graces came from Her hands).

Our Lady's Message of April 7, 1994
Through Gianna Talone Sullivan

My dear little children, praise be Jesus!

I would like all of you to know that living God's love may seem to
be a mystery, but will not remove you from the gift of your
humanness.

The mystery of His love allows you the freedom to be the human
being He created.

God loves you as you are.

Please first recognize His love for you in your humanness.

That is how you are brought to fulfillment and union in the Triune
God.

Please be who you are and live in God's love.

Live life in God, for God, and love one another in God and for
God.

Keep in mind My words to you on moral values, deception and purity.

Peace cannot exist as long as killings of all sorts continue and ways of demoralization occur.

You are all called to live a perfection of love through purity, fidelity and wholeness.

Please heed My words of truth, for there will be no choice other than to live a time of great difficulty.

This difficult time is extremely close to being unveiled and will be a result of My Son's mercy.

Begin gathering necessary resources now to sustain you in living the way of love.

I wish for all My children to have a time of preparation and opportunity to choose life through His love.

Peace and love, little children.

Thank you for responding to My call. Ad Deum.

Our Lady's Message of April 14, 1994
through Gianna Talone Sullivan

My dear little children, praise be Jesus!

My little ones, so many of My children are scattering instead of joining together in prayer.

The commitment to prayer I have invited you to is life long.

It cannot be temporary or only in the time of need.

Do you not see that through the gift of prayer you are able to express the many virtues My Son graces you?

Prayer is simple, but I cannot help you unless you take on the commitment as I have invited you several times.

It is a **daily** commitment of time to be with My Son, desiring change and challenge.

It is listening in openness.

My Son speaks to all, even in silence.

My little, little children, realize how patient My Son is with you.

Please, how many warnings have I presented throughout the ages that have been softened or even mitigated because of prayer, response and My Son's patience?

Take seriously My call to prayer, unity and change.

Perhaps you have become too comfortable with My presence.

Please recognize the gift He has given to you by allowing Me to be here, and **please** respond.

It is because of My Son's mercy and love for you.

Do not neglect Him or take lightly His requests, for the time will arrive quickly when you will wish to hear My words and will no longer.

My Son loves you.

Please do not become lax in prayer.

Please live His words to the best of your ability.

Please, please, please pray with all your heart.

Peace.

Thank you for responding to My call. Ad Deum.

Our Lady's Message of April 21, 1994
through Gianna Talone Sullivan

My dear little children, praise be Jesus!

My little ones, please surrender to My Son.

If you would surrender unto His mercy in your misery, you would see His wondrous works unveil.

My words are simple and I wish to help you be happy and free, but you need to surrender and trust God.

If you are miserable, then the opportunity to surrender to My Son's mercy exists at this present moment.

Do not delay.

The wonders of God will unfold before you and you all can live in the glory of God in harmony.

But if you do not lay your miseries at the foot of the cross, embracing who you are and your need for His mercy, you will continue to live in a world of division and destruction.

Call on Jesus.

Call on His mercy.

Surrender to His mercy.

Trust in Him and see the wonders of God unfold.

There is no time such as the present to accept God's mercy.

Please, children, accept God's merciful love through surrendering
and trusting in Him.
Thank you for responding to My call.

(Our Blessed Mother prayed over everyone
and blessed us, especially the priests.)

Our Lady's Message of April 28, 1994
through Gianna Talone Sullivan

My dear little children, praised be Jesus!
My little ones, you are so consumed with the fear of My authentic-
ity that you are failing to see how the Lord in His humility has
allowed Me to be here with you.
Focus on Jesus in the Eucharist and trust in Him.
Fear God, that you might not offend Him in self pride and self
righteousness.
Be humble, love Him, implore His mercy, adore Him in the most
Blessed Sacrament.
But do not fear whether you are being deceived in trying to au-
thenticate My presence.
I belong to God. You belong to God.
Remember, a house not of God will divide itself.
Put your fears to rest and hope in the resurrected Christ!
There is no time for fear. There is time for change.
You are all novices in the knowledge of His most merciful love.
Remove yourself and allow My Son to be your God.
Remove the idolatry you have formed of yourself and placed higher
than He.
He is your God.
And I have been allowed to come here to implore you to focus on
Him, trust Him and return back to Him.
I plead with you not to advocate abortion as a form of population
control.
My little ones, please notice the destruction and desolation and
desecration which results from destroying the temple of God.
Life is your gift. Life is a treasure and not a burden.

Abuse it and My Son will take it away from you.

Please heed My warning in His name.

Please pray before My Son in the most Blessed Sacrament and implore His mercy and grace to enlighten you with His truth of life.

Peace, my little ones and thank you for responding to this most serious call.

Ad Deum.

Our Lady's Message of May 5, 1994
through Gianna Talone Sullivan

My dear children, praise be Jesus!

My little, little children, pray that God's mercy make you clean and turn you away from your sinful ways.

You are little children acting as if you are all knowing and powerful in God's love.

Return to God in littleness and depend on Him to lead you.

Pray before Him in the most Blessed Sacrament for truth of your deceitful ways so that you will be able to repent in humility and be made whole.

My Son loves you and I wish to help you and save you from walking towards a life of human destruction.

Allow Me to bring you to My Son.

Allow Me to present your beauty of a child.

In order to do this, you must humbly submit to changing your deceitful ways of power, reputation, acceptance of man, success for your glory, to that which belongs to God.

Return to God and at all costs seek to be obedient to Him.

Only those who risk even the chance of hardship for God, in obedience to following the truth of His word, are true commanders in His army of love.

It is time you put into action your love for Him.

You must be willing to give everything up for God to be true lovers of Christ.

Peace, little ones.

Peace.

Our Lady's Message of May 12, 1994
through Gianna Talone Sullivan

My dear little children, praise be Jesus!

My little ones, pray with all your heart during these next nine days that you be enlightened by the gifts of the Holy Spirit.

Pray always for God's gift of gratitude.

It is in gratitude to Him that you shall receive more gifts.

Always be thankful for God's goodness and love.

My Son loves you tremendously.

He has not forsaken you.

Be whole in Him.

Be little children.

To be little is to simply "be" and love God, trusting in Him.

Be totally dependent on Him as a child.

You utilize your intellect far more than your heart.

Pray with your heart. Process everything through your heart.

You are relying on your mind instead of your heart, especially in reflection, which causes resistance and lack of joy.

God's grace is made abundant to you.

His way is simple.

It is time you pray for fortitude and surrender to God's will at all times.

Procure your relationship now with God as a dependent child, in littleness and in gratitude.

Thank you, little ones, for responding to My call.

My blessings.

Peace.

Our Lady's Message of May 19, 1994
through Gianna Talone Sullivan

My dear little children, praise be Jesus!

My Son, who has given everything to the Father for love of you, even His life, asks that you give everything to Him, for love of Him.

What, little children, are you willing to risk for love of God?

Many of My children currently say they are willing to risk all for God, but at this present time only a small percentage of the world's population are truly willing.

Are you one who will soon turn away from My Son and deny Him?

My little children, there is no time left.

You are no longer listening to My words and it is almost too late.

The brilliance of the moon has begun to reflect that of bloodshed.

I **urge** you to pray like you have never prayed before.

Pray and ask the Holy Spirit for counsel, understanding, fear of God, fortitude, piety, wisdom and knowledge of His truth.

I want to help you, little ones.

I love you.

You must change right now and live in God's peace or it will be too late.

Do not fear, but **LISTEN** to My words and unite in the family, pray and love.

Simplify your lives and live for God, who loves you.

Bless you, little ones.

I remain with you.

Peace.

Our Lady's Message of May 26, 1994
through Gianna Talone Sullivan

My dear little children, praise be Jesus!

My little ones, if you had knowledge of salvation, you would be freed from fear and from your enemies.

The Holy Spirit, through His gift of charity, gives you understanding and knowledge.

He enlightens you to rejoice in God. He sanctifies you.

Those who live in the Holy Spirit live in gratitude for graces received.

I desire to help you and intercede for you, but you must LISTEN to My words and respond to My call.

Currently, the vast majority of My children whom I desire to help are hearing only what they choose to hear.

Please **LISTEN** to ALL My words of truth.

You cannot only recognize My plea, but must respond through acceptance of My words and living them.

I tell you again, little ones, you must be willing to risk all for **love** of God.

My Son freed you by giving all to God for love of you.

He has given everything to you. He has provided for you.

But now, you are not willing to give back to God what He has given to you, because you are slaves to fear and do not trust My Son.

How can I help you if you select the words I speak which you choose to hear?

Listen, little children. Listen to My motherly call and respond.

Do not be afraid to give yourself totally to God.

He will always provide for you and fill you with joy.

Do not be slaves to fear and materialism.

If you give yourself unconditionally to My Son, you will allow Me to be a Mother who will provide the best for Her children.

Peace, little ones. Thank you for responding to My call.

(Our Lady was crying. She blessed everyone,
especially the little children.)

Our Lady's Message of June 2, 1994
through Gianna Talone Sullivan

My dear little children, praise be Jesus who loves you!

Praise be to the Father who loves you!

Praise be to the Holy Spirit who loves and feeds your soul!

My little ones, you must dive into My most Immaculate Heart **immediately**!

I wish for you all to be consecrated to My Immaculate Heart and to be safe and free!

Please, little ones, I can no longer hold back the hand of My Son from the sorrow incurred on His Sacred Heart.

Little, little children, you are not listening to My words.

You are not living My messages.

Do you not see how I desire to help you?

There are few who trust in God.
There are few living in His faith.
Please, little children, I urgently ask you to heed My call.
Adore Jesus in the most Blessed Sacrament.
Pray to the Father and trust in His most tender love.
I love you, little ones and I have given you many messages to assist you in knowing His truth.
Live the messages and pray you will not be tested, but free and happy.
I bless you, little children and thank you for responding to My call.

(Our Lady said, My dear beloved priests, unite together, for a sword is soon to pierce your heart. Dive into My Immaculate Heart.)

Our Lady's Message of June 9, 1994
through Gianna Talone Sullivan

My dear little children, praise be Jesus!
My little ones, if you only **hear** the word of God, you are not justified in His sight.
Only those who observe and live His word will be justified.
You will not be justified through your works, but on the basis of your faith.
It is your faith and trust in God which will make you righteous.
You need to live the messages of God.
Live His word. You cannot only hear it.
You cannot wear an external image of holiness.
God sees all things.
It is the **spirit** of your works and your living **faith** in God which will make you holy.
My little ones, all your hidden works will be judged.
You cannot hide from God.
All good and evil will be weeded out and to everyone will be revealed the truth of their incentives and state of faith.
Graces flow out from My hands little children, desiring to help you.

I love you. My Son loves you.

He is loving and merciful.

Children, lastly I ask you to pray for and support all My beloved priests.

The sword is soon to pierce their hearts.

Pray for your priests, bishops and cardinals.

Pray for unity and peaceful resolutions between priests, bishops and cardinals.

I bless you all, little children. Know God loves you.

I have pointed the way to My Son. It is **now** your choice.

Peace, and thank you for responding to My call.

Our Lady's Message of June 16, 1994
through Gianna Talone Sullivan

My dear little children, praise be Jesus!

This time period designated by My Son is the last period in which I will be allowed to come to you, My little children, throughout the world.

Please heed My words, for I am a loving Mother who desires to help you.

Little, little children, pray! pray! pray! pray for peace.

Pray within your families.

Unity, compassion and forgiveness are fruits from prayer in the family, and I have told you that you cannot have a pure heart unless you forgive.

Be obedient to My beloved Pope and support My beloved priests.

Serve My Son in joy and in freedom by contributing to the needs of others.

Exercise hospitality.

Rejoice in hope, endure in affliction and persevere in prayer.

Do not look for revenge on others, but practice mercy.

Mercy is the missing link to loving.

My Son loves you, the Father loves you and desires you to recognize love.

He is Love.

I take your petitions to the Sacred Heart of My Son and remind
you to implore and invite the Holy Spirit to sanctify you.
Thank you, little children, for your response to My call.
I bless you in the name of My Son, who has allowed Me to be here.
Peace. Ad Deum.

Our Lady's Message of June 23, 1994
through Gianna Talone Sullivan

My dear little children, praise be Jesus!
My little ones, please do not judge others.
Be kind and loving.
How you judge others reflects how you perceive yourself and would
judge yourself.
Focus on My Son.
Please do not be distracted.
If you are uncharitable, you deny the love of Jesus and cannot wear
the armor as a true follower of Him.
To be in union with God, you must pray, be charitable, be obedient
and serve the needs of all through love.
This requires faith and this union with God will never be destroyed.
Little children, God loves you very much and desires that you know
Him.
Please be open to His love.
Be eager to present yourself as acceptable to God.
Please do not cause disgrace for others.
Satan is desperately attempting to cause division.
Anger, hatred, resentfulness, jealousy, malice and premeditated
attempts to strip others of respect, dignity and self esteem are
the poisonous venoms to evil.
Silence is the shield and love the sword to battle evil.
I invite you to live ways of charity, patience, kindness and love
towards one another.
When you hurt others, you truly are hurting yourself.
Peace, little ones and thank you for responding to My call.
Ad Deum.

Our Lady's Message of June 30, 1994
through Gianna Talone Sullivan

My dear children, praise be Jesus!

My little ones, humble yourself unto God.

Those who humble themselves are exalted.

My Son lifts the lowly to high places.

Pray for humility like God.

Surrender and trust in Him.

Remember, it is not your works that give God glory, but your living faith and the **spirit** of your works.

Use integrity to accomplish the works of God in His love.

Integrity is honesty, sincerity and wholeness.

Wholeness is abandoning yourself to live in union with God by doing His will.

If you are humble in His sight, you will know His will, for you will know Him.

Love is simple.

Love is patience.

Be patient with yourself as you surrender and grow in His love.

God loves you and is tender, merciful and patient.

He desires that the fruits of His love exemplify charity, joy and tranquility of peace in your life.

Virtues and abundant graces will flow from His most Sacred Heart if you will allow them.

My little children, allow God to be God.

I am here to tell you God does exist and you are invited to His banquet through love and mercy.

Please accept His invitation with a "yes" of loving.

Peace, and thank you for responding to My call.

Ad Deum.

Our Lady's Message to the World of July 7, 1994
through Gianna Talone Sullivan

My dear little children, praise be Jesus!

My little ones, I desire all to be united to My Son.

I desire all people to be happy and filled with joy and freedom.

There are so many of My children who suffer because they have kept their distance from God.

There are also many of My children who **joyfully** suffer in union with My Son as victims of His love.

The cross is the connection to suffering **with** joy and love in union with My Son.

Those who carry the cross of My Son are co-redemptors of His love through His salvation and mercy.

Do not fear the cross.

His cross is sweetness, charity, meekness, wisdom, justice, mercy and truth.

Join together little children and unite with My Son in the joyful sufferings of love of your cross.

Pray for all My dear little ones who have chosen to keep their distance from God.

It is not God's desire they suffer the sufferings of a world without His love.

The suffering of love is one of joy, freedom, surrendering, abandonment, even though painful many times.

This is due to sanctification, purification, wholeness and becoming LOVE.

Jesus is LOVE. He desires you to be Him, TO BE LOVE.

Please do not fear the joy of His cross He desires to share with you.

Pray. Pray. Pray.

You will come to understand and love the cross in His love the closer you come to His light.

Pray and you will desire His cross as He desires to **gift** you with it.

It is not the cross of the suffering of the world, but the suffering of LOVE.

Thank you, little children, for responding to My call and peace be with you. Ad Deum.

Our Lady's Message of July 14, 1994
through Gianna Talone Sullivan

My dear little children, praise be Jesus!

Thank you for coming to pray with reverence for God, who awaits you in love and is the giver of all that is good.

God in His mercy and fidelity will not forsake you.

He is the lover of all that is good.

He is your creator. He is Love.

Little children, you also must love and have a mutual love for one another.

You are His heirs to His inheritance.

Be sincere and love one another with mutual affection.

Look to do good, not evil.

Be patient with each other's failings and live in harmony with one another.

It is in God alone that you become victorious.

That is why I invite you, little children, to turn to God in child-like ways, to pray and to live in His merciful love, and to have a mutual affection towards one another.

Please do not try the patience of others.

You must all share in the gift of patience and self- denial to be sole heirs of God's righteousness.

My children, you know to pray. Do not delay.

Take the initiative, in God's grace, and pray.

Especially My little, little ones, please pray, little children, every day for your parents, family and for peace.

The little children shall be instruments of salvation through prayer, the Rosary and love.

Do not rejoice over the failings of others, but in meekness and in love, show mercy.

Rejoice in what is good, not in what is evil. Pray!

Blessings of God, My little ones.

Peace, and thank you for responding to My call. Ad Deum.

Our Lady's Message to the World of July 21, 1994
through Gianna Talone Sullivan

My dear little children, praise be Jesus!

Little children, success in life should not be enmeshed in performance which is only temporary, but should be in God.

Do not see God solely as an instrument to your happiness, but see Him as the intrinsic way of life.

Invest in a success that is of God.

Do you not know that all you have has been given to you as a gift from God and not of your own merit?

How long will you continue to be complacent with the goodness of God?

Little children, all you do must be done for God, in God and because of God's eternal love for you.

All the accomplishments you achieve in your earthly life without Him will only be short lived, because you can do nothing without Him.

Only His works are perfect.

Seek to please God.

He is infinite and you are infinitely important to Him.

You have kept your distance from Him and as a result are imperfect in love and weak in virtue.

If you return to God, He will lovingly mold you in His love, to love and be love.

Place God at the center of your life by surrendering all of your attachments, concerns, fears and manipulating ways to God.

Trust in His Divine mercy and love.

Interiorly release all your control to God.

Be little children, **dependent** totally on God, and be free.

Bless you, little ones.

I take your petitions to My Son who is One with the Father.

I keep nothing for Myself. All is given to Him.

Praise be God forever!

Peace. Thank you for responding to My call. Ad Deum.

(Our Lady blessed everyone and came with
two baby angels. She prayed over everybody.)

Our Lady's Message of July 28, 1994
through Gianna Talone Sullivan

My dear little children, praise be Jesus!

Little ones, please love one another with a pure heart.

Accept all people in their weakness.

Be patient.

Love yourself as you are and love others as they are.

God loves you as you are.

Do not place limitations on your love.

Do not restrict your love based off the spirituality of another person.

Do not love less because someone does not meet your standards.

Love all.

Do what is good to others.

Only God knows the deepest incentives of the heart.

God is infinite.

Love unconditionally.

Seek to please God and to love as He loves in purity and in fidelity to His goodness.

Conversion of heart, sinfulness and uncharitable actions are changed through love and mercy.

If you fail, please try again.

Great salvation comes to the weak through sincere effort in loving.

Even in your sinfulness, as you love and try to live in purity, you do not fail, but you are strengthened in humility and in charity.

I bless you, little children, in the name of My Son and I hear your plea.

I take your petitions to My Son's most Sacred Heart.

Thank you for responding to My call.

Ad Deum.

Our Lady's Message of August 4, 1994
through Gianna Talone Sullivan

My dear little children, praise be Jesus!

Little ones, I thank you for your prayers for your country and I ask you to continue to pray for your country and for My beloved Pope.

I invite all the little, little children to be consecrated to My Immaculate Heart and to pray every day with their friends and families.

There is so much that can be mitigated through prayer.

Pray for peace in the world, in your families and in your souls.

My Son has tremendous love for you and does not wish for you to live in turmoil.

He desires peace.

Peace can exist through prayer and love, but it is necessary that you respond in action.

Please respond by being the fabric of His love.

Response to My call of love and mercy through unity, prayer, penance and fasting, are important factors which can ward off wars and spoken chastisements.

I desire to help you, all My children of this world, but you must allow me by responding to My Son's plea.

He has outlined the path of truth.

Give to My Son all your pain and all that you hold bound in your heart.

Turn to Him.

You can be free in God's love.

I bless you, little ones, and know I am here to bring you hope.

Please respond to My call.

I take your petitions to My Son's most Sacred Heart.

Peace.

AD DEUM.

Our Lady's Message of August 11,1994
through Gianna Talone Sullivan

My dear little children, praise be Jesus!

Little children, dedicate yourselves in thankfulness to God.

God's peace must be in your hearts.

Praise Him with your hearts as well as your lips.

I desire you to be close to God, free and happy.

I desire for you to live in His joy.

Only this can be accomplished through prayer, surrendering to God's direction, and giving Him His recompense of true sorrow for your sins.

Satan is trying to discourage you.

He would like you to believe there is no need for penance or faithfulness in fidelity to God.

Please, little children, cast off the burden of your sins and allow God to make for you a clean heart and spirit—one of love.

My Son does not take pleasure in the death of a soul.

He desires all to live in Him.

Therefore, little children, over all virtues put on love.

Love will bind all other virtues and make them perfect.

For God is Love and He is perfect, for He is Yahweh, your Emmanuel.

Bless you, little ones, in the name of Jesus.

I take your petitions to Him who has allowed Me to be here with you.

Thank you for responding to My call.

Peace. AD DEUM.

Our Lady's Message of August 18, 1994
through Gianna Talone Sullivan

My dear little children, praise be Jesus!

Little children, take the time to enjoy and appreciate with gratitude all the gifts and blessings My Son has granted and betrothed unto you.

Believe with all your heart in your salvation and immerse yourself in His love.

God loves you, little ones.

Live in total confidence of His love, knowing He will take care of you.

He will not forsake you, for you have been called by name.

Love one another.

Have no fear.

Trust in God.

Be dependent on God's love as little children.

Please do not form negative opinions or pass judgement on one another.

Be aware of your own actions and love unconditionally.

Focus on God and your own relationship with Him.

85

Strive to serve Him in humility.

You cannot serve God when love is lacking.

If you harbor emotions of bitterness, anger, jealousy, hatred or complacency towards one another, you are unable to serve God in humility.

To serve God, there must be love, for God is Love.

I bless you, little children, in the name of Jesus and I thank you for responding to My call.

Peace. AD DEUM.

Our Lady's Message of August 25,1994
through Gianna Talone Sullivan

My dear little children, praise be Jesus!

As your Mother, little ones, I bless you in the name of Jesus and encourage you to hope in Jesus.

Please do not neglect the divine reality in your own lives.

Add to the wonders of God in your fidelity to Him.

In simpleness, gentleness and in the quietness of prayer, God will fulfill His divine plan in your lives.

God's good works unveil in the simplicity of love.

Trust in His promise and be confident that He will fulfill all of His design for you in proper time.

Be filled with His joy, for you are infinitely important to Him.

I love you, little children.

Please do not lose your focus.

There is hope for all people of the world through prayer and mercy.

Be kind and charitable so that God's good works and fruits of His promise will surface.

You prevent His love to surface when you do not allow mercy, compassion and honesty to be an integral part of your lives.

Less speech and more silence of prayer will reveal the truth and allow the Divinity of peace to enter.

Peace, little ones.

Thank you for responding to My call.

AD DEUM.

Our Lady's Message of September 1,1994
through Gianna Talone Sullivan

My dear little children, praise be Jesus!

Little children, help your neighbor through love and gentleness.

Please remember that every man has faults.

Your neighbor may have faults, but there are also defects in you.

Detest sin, but love the sinner!

Be patient with the faults of your neighbor.

You can overcome your burdens and difficulties through the grace I obtain for you from God.

The grace from God may not always do away with difficulties, but it will help you bear them.

Your walk in the life of holiness has many sacrifices.

Utilize every opportunity and occasion of such sacrifices to glorify God through love and gentleness.

If your neighbors displease you, do not complain, for it will not accelerate their correction.

It will not be helpful in the situation.

Please pray for the virtue of gentleness and the spirit of peace.

Ask Jesus to help you so that you may be granted the glorious title of "child of God."

Live in the Spirit's love.

All who live in the Spirit are called children of God.

Bless you, little children, in the name of Jesus who loves you as a child and who is patient.

Be merciful and mercy shall be yours.

Thank you for responding to My call.

Peace. Ad Deum.

Our Lady's Message of September 8, 1994
through Gianna Talone Sullivan

My dear little children, praise be Jesus!

My little ones, I am the Immaculate Conception, the spouse of the Holy Spirit.

Your Jesus is of My flesh and blood and I cherish the wonder of
life.
My son lived this gift of life from God to its fullest, and He desires
all to live life with all its wonders, in Him.
The gift is life.
Give yourself to God in this life on earth.
Devote time to prayer and prepare yourself to receive the graces
God desires to give you.
Do not wait until the moment of need arises or you will be too
exhausted from the world's yoke to carry the yoke of God.
As a child, your thoughts, affections and heart should be conse-
crated to God.
It is never too late to be a servant of God.
However weak you may think your soul is, Jesus will always find
joy to come to it.
Make every effort to improve.
Receive Holy Eucharist so Jesus will find great joy in dwelling in
you.
Profit by the remedy offered in Jesus as the "bread of life."
Do not use an excuse of fear to stay away from Jesus.
Surrender to "love" and strive to live in His love to its fullest,
living life, living love.
Bless you little ones.
My gift to you is My Son.
Thank you for responding to My call.
AD DEUM.

Our Lady's Message of September 15, 1994
through Gianna Talone Sullivan

My dear little children, praise be Jesus!
I am your Mother, who shares in your joys and your sorrows.
Please remember, little ones, before the sword struck you, it first
pierced My Immaculate Heart.
A mother does not allow her children to suffer alone, for a mother
who loves shares in that sorrow of her children.
I share your sorrow and I take your suffering to God.

Offer all your suffering, little children, for purity, peace and charity in the world.

As a gentle Mother, I caress your tender hearts, which have been submerged in the complexity of life's burden imposed by man.

If you only return to the simplicity of God, you can be free in love and live in peace.

Pray, pray, pray, little ones.

Pray that you be open to the truth outlined by My Son and be able to decide for God, whatever the cost.

Only then can your sorrow turn into joy.

I love you, My little children.

Remember, you are infinitely important to God.

Please decide now for God, little ones, for your destiny depends on your decision.

You have a choice.

You have a free will to decide for God and be consecrated to His word.

I bless you, little children, and I thank you for responding to My call.

Ad Deum.

Our Lady's Message of September 22, 1994
through Gianna Talone Sullivan

My dear little children, praise be Jesus!

Little ones, live your life to the fullest and do whatever is necessary to seek the kingdom of God.

The next life is a different life than the one you live currently.

Strive for the Beatific Vision of eternal happiness.

God in His goodness invites all to live in His glory.

Living your life now in the love of God is the only chance you have to solidify your security in the future.

Decide for God now.

Your decision will mark your destiny.

Little children, God does exist and evil does exist.

Your loved ones in Heaven pray for the light to illuminate the darkness which has consumed much of the world.

It is My mission that the world know the truth and for no soul to be deceived.

I desire for all to belong to God.

Seek the kingdom of God, little ones.

Work in perfect humility and meekness.

Live life with all its wonders to its fullest.

Do your best to serve one another in love and to receive graciously.

God loves you, little ones, and I bless you in His name.

Peace.

Thank you for responding to My call.

Ad Deum.

Our Lady's Message of September 29, 1994
through Gianna Talone Sullivan

My dear little children, praise be Jesus!

Little children, My words are simple in the love of God.

Listen with your heart.

On this special feast day, reflect how holiness is the basis of dignity.

Holiness does not depend on extraordinary gifts with which you are graced.

It is a direct response to your fidelity in your duties to God.

Your deeds must be holy if they are to be esteemed by God.

It is your response to your gifts and what you do with them for God that merits His rewards.

It is not the gift itself, but your response to your gift.

Your constant fidelity in persevering in faithfulness to God's will distinguishes you under His grace.

It is your response to the grace from God, little children, and cooperation, which makes you holy.

Seek to imitate Jesus every day.

Ask Him for the grace to be able to imitate an aspect of Him.

Jesus loves you so much that He gave you the true examples of patience, humility, obedience, meekness and piety.

Ponder His modesty and meekness that marked His words.

Reflect and examine your own inclinations and sentiments and pray
for the grace of God to be bestowed on you, that your works
may be holy and filled with dignity.
Bless you, little ones, and thank you for responding to My call.
Ad Deum.

Our Lady's Message of October 6, 1994
through Gianna Talone Sullivan

My dear little children, praise be Jesus!
My little ones, please do not be afraid or confused.
My plan for you is great.
It is one of joy and freedom.
Unite with Me in prayer for My plan.
Little children, it is very important that you continually give of
yourself in God's love to one another.
Do not avoid your neighbor, but genuinely be loving and kind.
Pray for the grace of God to help you.
You must remember that you are all novices.
No matter what spiritual level you feel you have achieved, it is the
beginning of an eternal walk of intimacy with God.
Only God visualizes the plan in its entirety and you, little children,
must remain dependent on Him, trusting in His Divine will.
As God's will unfolds daily, please do not be sad or confused when
you realize His will may not be what you have planned.
Remain open and accept His plan for you with unconditional love.
God's works are wondrous.
He confuses the proud and exalts the humble.
Surrender to His will in peace.
It will result in eternal happiness, for God will remain faithful to
His promise.
Bless you, little children.
I take your petitions to the Sacred Heart of Jesus.
Bless you!
Thank you for responding to My call.
Ad Deum.

Our Lady's Message of October 13, 1994
through Gianna Talone Sullivan

My dear little children, praise be Jesus!

Little children, the time is arriving when every man, woman and child on this earth will have to make a decision for or against God.

Please do not be afraid to decide for God or to take a risk for God.

There is nothing to fear.

Trust in God's loving care.

He will protect you.

No matter what the circumstance, God loves you, for God is Love.

Put to rest your fears and give everything to God now by deciding for God now.

You will experience the lighthearted joy and freedom of love.

Reflect on what is love.

Do not focus on bloodshed or impending doom, which will distract you and cause you to fear.

Rather, focus on love, serenity, simpleness, kindness and freedom.

Focus on God, trust in Him, and surrender to Him in submissiveness by accepting His will.

Your fear will dissipate and your focus will result in an action of love and prayer.

Little children, deciding for God is trusting in God.

Taking a risk for God is to leap with unconditional love towards Him in His call of mercy for you, a mission placed in your heart by God.

Please, little children, decide now for God.

You will **never** regret your decision.

Peace.

Thank you for responding to My call. Ad Deum.

Our Lady's Message of November 3, 1994
through Gianna Talone Sullivan

My dear little children, praise be Jesus!

Little children, glory belongs to God alone, because all virtue comes from Him.

Preserve a humble heart and do not follow the quest for the world's glory and the esteem of people through the world's honor.

Seek God alone and aspire to a glory that is solid and whole in love.

Little children, have an unfailing confidence in Me, your Mother.

I shall intercede for you and all who desire to return to God's service.

I am the refuge of all sinners.

God has never said "no" to My prayer.

Do not continue to live in sin.

Turn to My Son, who loves and pardons offenses.

Put your trust in Him.

Have hope and pray!

Draw near, little children.

I will not reject you, but will intercede for you and win the grace of forgiveness and strength for you.

I welcome you with love. My Son welcomes you with love.

Love and compassion overflow from the covenant of our hearts.

Learn the spirit of love and forgiveness that the Gospel prescribes.

When you do reparation, you are disposed to allowing Our Hearts to be united with you.

Bless you, little ones, on this day that My Son has allowed Me to come to you and to this center of My Immaculate Heart.

Peace. Ad Deum.

Our Lady's Message of November 10, 1994
through Gianna Talone Sullivan

My dear little children, praise be Jesus!

Little children, I ask you to have confidence in Me, your Mother of Joy.

I will intercede for you to God, present you, and plead for your cause on your behalf.

If it is God's will, all you ask will come to pass, for My prayer has never been refused by God.

Do not come to Me only in times of need, when difficulties arise, or on feast days only.

Allow Me to dispense the graces God has willed for you at all times.

The loving tenderness of God has deigned that I be the dispenser of all graces and the Church seeks My intercession continually.

Please, I invite you to do the same. My Son awaits your love.

Please do not restrict the graces you are able to receive by restricting the entrance of God's love from lack of trust and confidence.

As the Church has recourse to Me, please do so also.

Let your conduct be as Mine—all embracing, sweet and affectionate.

Come to Me always and in all your spiritual and temporal needs.

I will not fail you, for I am your Mother leading you to My Son.

Do not be unsure of My good will for you.

I desire you to be perfect in God's love.

I will take you to Jesus in the form that is irresistible.

Jesus in turn will take you to the Father.

It is the most direct and quickest path to My Son and to the Father, for My love is pure, simple and free from sin.

My little children, God is mercy, God is love, and you all are invited to live in union with the Triune God.

You are all invited to Mercy. You are all invited to Love.

Come, little children, come.

The abyss of all blessings is awaiting you in His love.

I bless you, little ones, and take your petitions to My Son's most Sacred Heart, where joy, mercy and charity reside.

Peace. Thank you for responding to My call.

Ad Deum.

Our Lady's Message of November 17, 1994
through Gianna Talone Sullivan

My dear little children, praise be Jesus!

Little children, no matter how great your suffering is in this life, know there is nothing that is equivalent to the suffering of not loving My Son.

There is no happiness unless it is in His love.
The love of God is everything.
It is your joy, your life, your food.
Your treasure is in the love of Jesus.
In His love, you are truly rich.
There is no wealth greater than the wealth of God's love.
There is no gem worth more or that captures the precision of per-
 fection than the love of Jesus.
I invite you, little children, to this great treasure of His love.
In His love there is a blessing which no one nor anything can supple-
 ment.
Please take My words of invitation seriously.
Dive into the abyss of My Son's most Sacred Heart and be love.
There you will be nourished and comforted.
There you will rest in His peace.
I love you, My little children, and take your petitions to My Son.
I bless you in His name and I thank you for responding to My call.
Ad Deum.

Our Lady's Message of December 1, 1994
through Gianna Talone Sullivan

My dear little children, praise be Jesus!
Little children, pray with your heart, listen with your heart, speak
 with your heart, think with your heart, and see with your heart.
My Son loves you.
Hear My words with your heart.
What does it mean to you that My Son loves you?
Process through your heart all My words and words you speak to
 others.
This is the time when My Son is awaiting the hour to arrive, when
 His joy can come into your hearts.
This is the time for you to keep vigil and wait for joy.
My Son is the joy of your heart.
Await Him in anticipation through prayer.
Keep watch for Him.
Never lose sight that your victory results in His love and mercy.

Joy of God is coming for those who seek Him with all their hearts.
Joy is coming for those who invite Him into their hearts.
Pray, keep vigil, pray and wait for He is coming to fill you with love and peace.
I bless you, little ones, and take your petitions to God the Father.
Peace, and thank you for responding to My call.
Ad Deum.

(Our Blessed Mother blessed everyone ,
especially the priests.)

Our Lady's Message of December 8, 1994
through Gianna Talone Sullivan

My dear little children, praise be Jesus!
Little ones, to love God is to soar into the heavenly bliss of matrimony.
The insult of love on the natural affection must be caught in the rapture of God's holy love.
There He draws you to His breast and holds you tight.
The heavenly court of angels sing the glorious hymns of praise and adoration.
Come, all you My little children, come to the Father of love.
You are called by name to receive His zeal of love.
Little ones, face your challenges and obstacles of life and rise above them by working continuously in the field of love.
Meet your offenders without fear and press for unity through love.
Do not be afraid to risk your honor and never cease working in the field of love and service for God.
There is much work that needs to be done in the harvest of love.
I need an army who will face challenges with love in fidelity to God and who will surrender in faithfulness to Him.
The battle against truth strikes, but the power of persistence, perseverance and love results in victory, freedom and peace.
Bless you, little ones, and thank you for responding to My call.
Ad Deum.

Our Lady's Message of December 15, 1994
through Gianna Talone Sullivan

My dear little children, praise be Jesus!

Little ones, the day of joy and promise of God is approaching.

Live as if today were your last.

Be at peace in your tribulations and be confident in God's promise.

Trust in His love.

He will swiftly come to your aid and free you from all despair.

Rejoice because of His love for you.

You belong to Him.

God does not cause harm or fear, but protects and comforts the afflicted.

Sing joyfully to God your strength; acclaim the God of Jacob!

Little ones, every day of your life should be lived for God in offering.

It should be filled with the Christmas song of love and adoration for His kindness and faithfulness.

His vows are never broken.

No matter the circumstance, your heart of love should be dedicated in resignation to God's will and filled with joy.

Look to the glorious day of meeting Him face to face with heart-filled longing and joyful offerings of praise.

I love you, little ones and invite you to join Me in joyful songs of praise to our Emmanuel.

Peace, little ones.

I take your petitions in love.

Blessings of God, little ones.

Ad Deum.

Our Lady's Message of December 22, 1994
through Gianna Talone Sullivan

My dear little children, praise be Jesus!

Little ones, an unshakable confidence in My Son's promise is the power which fulfills it.

Trust in His words of love and truth spoken to you with confidence.

God will not harm you.

If your requests are not answered according to your desire, it is because God has planned a greater outcome for your happiness.

God's will and plan for your life is made perfect in His love.

Have confidence in His mercy and humbly submit to His Holy will.

God sanctifies and purifies His chosen ones.

Be at peace, little children.

Know you are never alone.

Have confidence in God's great love for you and be dependent on His care.

I love you, My little ones, and desire to help you, but you must trust and place your confidence in God's love for you.

Please do not restrict the graces He desires to give you.

Rejoice, His favor rests on you.

You belong to Him, rejoice!

Peace, little ones.

I bless you in His name of Love.

I take your petitions to the Father.

Thank you for responding to My call.

Ad Deum.

Our Lady's Message of December 29, 1994
through Gianna Talone Sullivan

My dear little children, praise be Jesus!

Little children, I desire to help you obtain great graces from God and for you to receive great joy, but you must respond to My requests.

Do not limit the works of God, please, little ones.

In order for the fruits of My Son to continue to unfold, it is most necessary that you utilize the sacrament of reconciliation more frequently and that you, My beloved priests, make it more available.

You cannot have a pure heart unless you recognize your sins and confess them with a contrite heart.

Too many of My children are receiving Holy Communion without purifying their hearts through the sacrament first.

It is deception if you think you have not sinned, for My Son sacrificed Himself for sinners.

I also encourage you to spend heart filled hours of prayer before My Son in the Most Blessed Sacrament.

I call all My youth to return to adoration of My Son.

These two facets must be exercised and be at the center of your journey towards holiness.

I love you, My little children, but if you do not listen to My requests and respond, you will limit God's graces which He wishes to abundantly give you.

Peace, little ones.

I bless you and thank you for responding to this call.

Ad Deum.

Our Lady's Message of January 5, 1995
through Gianna Talone Sullivan

My dear little children, praise be Jesus!

Little children, there are many people who know death as a moment of terror.

But those who are filled with the love of My Son know death of the body as a time of consolation and tremendous peace.

Do not be more afraid than to be more loving.

Maintaining a holy fear of God's judgement allows you to see yourself as you are, but always let hope and love overcome your fear.

God loves you very much and created your soul to love Him.

Do not grow weary in seeking to possess His eternal light through serving Him, loving Him and affectionately loving one another in the grace of God.

Be patient and trust in the gift of your faith.

Trust in My Son. Have faith in Him.

It is a great gift He has given to you.

To have faith is to live it through love, service and mercy, perseverance and endurance.

Remember, all who hold out to the end will escape eternal death.

I encourage you to have trust in your faith and to have trust in His love.

Anything that happens is a result of His love for you.

Nothing can unfold unless God allows, and God allows trials to unfold because He loves you and wants you to know the truth.

He wants you to see yourself as you are.

He wants you to see Him as He is. But God can only love.

Anger and hatred cannot come from Him for He is Love and can only love.

Nor does anger or hatred harm God.

Love and gentleness are virtues given to you so you will know how much God loves you.

Ponder My words, little ones, and be open and ready always to endure all trials, for this is how God graces you with virtues and self-knowledge.

I bless you, little ones, and invite you to love and to be kind and to persevere in all trials of faith.

Blessings, little ones, and peace.

Thank you for responding to My call. Ad Deum.

(Our Lady prayed over everyone for perseverance.
She was serious, but not somber--emanating **hope**.)

Our Lady's Message of January 12, 1995
through Gianna Talone Sullivan

My dear little children, praise be Jesus!

My little ones, seek to grow not in self-love, but in self-knowledge of the truth of My Son's Divinity.

Strive to give to your neighbors the unconditional love and charity which is so much needed.

Do not render service only when it proves profitable to your own self.

Render unconditional service through the love of My Son's most Sacred Heart.

Do you not realize that the amount of unconditional love, charity and service given to your neighbor is proportional to the amount of love you have for God?

Ponder My words and recognize the deception of self-love when service is rendered with conditions.

Your love is impure when you withdraw a charitable act because it does not prove profitable to yourself.

The more you love your neighbor unconditionally, the more you love God unconditionally, and the more graces will pour forth from My Son's most Sacred Heart.

Purity of heart is the cornerstone to perfection of His virtues.

You are all called, little children, to be like unto My Son, pure of heart, to love unconditionally and to render charitable service to one another.

Peace, little ones.

I bless you in the name of My Son, who has allowed Me to be here with you.

Thank you for responding to My call.

Ad Deum.

(Our Lady prayed over everyone. She also blessed the deacons and priests and altar boy. She took everyone's petitions and private prayers.)

Our Lady's Message of January 19, 1995
through Gianna Talone Sullivan

My dear little children, praise be Jesus!

Little ones, God's love is never failing.

His love is infinite and you are infinitely important to Him.

Seek to serve Him in perfection of His love.

Put aside self-love and the comforts of this world, which are temporary.

In place, put on the armor of His love through service, penance and prayer for peace.

God will never fail you when your motives stem from love of His eternal Word.

If you live for God and in God, your grief shall be turned into joy, a joy filled with perseverance and strength.

Seek to build up your neighbors in the love of God.

Be cautious not to judge actions, for you do not know fully the facts as you do not know fully yourself.

Pay attention to God's love and live seeking His Kingdom, for it is the only chance you have in this life.

Put aside restless thoughts and strive for a mental silence, emerged in the peace and love of God.

Remember, simpleness and little actions of love gain way to fulfilling greater works in God's love.

Pray, little ones, pray and be **little** children of God.

I bless you in God's love and thank you for responding to My call. Ad Deum.

Our Lady's Message of January 26, 1995
through Gianna Talone Sullivan

My dear little children, praise be Jesus.

Little ones take delight in the Lord.

To love God is to take delight in His Word.

Be free of all distracting situations by focusing on His Word and living it.

Take time to read and study Scripture.

Know and learn all about My Son's life.

In knowing My Son you will learn and come to know yourself.

You will be able to handle all distracting disturbances and all situations with love as Jesus taught.

You will live according to His Word and fulfill His desires according to His Divine Providence.

If you do not know God you cannot live His Word.

You cannot follow His life.

Therefore study and seek to be like My Son.

You will be free of distractions because you will be firmly planted in His Heart.

I love you, little children, and take your petitions to God who blesses you.

The Word of God is My delight. He is the Word.
The Word of God should be your delight. Is it?
Is Jesus your delight?
Joy is knowing My Savior Jesus is with Me always.
Joy is yours for those who desire to know Him.
Knowing Jesus is the first step to unconditional love and charity.
Peace, little ones. Peace.
Thank you for responding to My call.
Ad Deum.

Our Lady's Message of February 2,1995
through Gianna Talone Sullivan

My dear little children, praise be Jesus!
Little ones, fear is useless.
What is needed is trust in God.
Trust in Him at all times, in all instances, under all circumstances.
Trust yourself to Divine Providence.
God is with you.
God loves you.
Little children, praise Him for allowing your eyes to gaze on Him.
If you are intimately united to His most Sacred Heart you will tap
    the source of repentant tears in admonishment of your sins.
Seek to be cleansed of all your sins so that you will gain the joys of
    heaven.
Little children, there is too much gossip and mockery of one an-
    other.
Please be conscious of your words and opinions of one another.
You scorn and sneer at those who do not seem virtuous or guided
    by the same principles of eternal Wisdom.
Yet you have counted yourself among the righteous and pious.
You have become bold in expertizing false and true prophets.
Be reminded that none is infallable, even the prophets who have
    gained recognition of pious belief from the Church.
Be free of profane entanglement and be inspired by love of Jesus.
Look to God and love all people.
Consecrate all your affections and thoughts to God.

Live in peace of conscience and joy of God's love for you.
Do not reject anyone.
Love and care for all people.
I bless you, little ones, and take your petitions to My Son.
Peace.
Thank you for responding to My call. AD DEUM.

(Our Lady came carrying the infant Jesus in Her left arm
and holding a gold staff (rod) at an angle.The head of the rod
had brilliant ruby's shining forth from it. She was wearing
white and had a gold crown on Her head).

Our Lady's Message of February 9, 1995
through Gianna Talone Sullivan

My dear little children, praise be Jesus!
Little children, no servant is greater than his master.
You claim to belong to God but you contradict your claim from your lack of committment to daily family prayer accompanied by leading a disciplined life working towards a pure heart.
Purity of heart comes by Divine grace, however it also demands honest effort on your part in devoting your life to My Son.
You must continually work on conquering your self- love, mastering your passions, practicing patience, and doing penance.
You must do works of humble service and works of love for your neighbor.
You cannot call yourself a child of God unless you serve the Lord Jesus My Son.
Do you desire Him? Do you seek Him? Do you follow Him?
Do you honor Him? Do you trust Him?
My Son has kept His promise of all ages to His people.
He sacrificed His life for your salvation. He is merciful.
Yet there are so many who have lukewarm hearts.
These lukewarm hearts are the ones which afflict My Son's most Sacred Heart. They are disinterested and indifferent.
The temporal needs are far greater in their eyes than eternal needs.

Unless these lukewarm hearts practice prayer daily and exercise perseverance in trials, they will turn into cold stone hearts.

Please allow correction by My Son.

Stand firm in penance and hope to be angels of light.

Do not seek a tragic end, but seek God's mercy. He is THE LORD!

If you do not wish to accept My words of enlightenment and seek by the grace of God to change your lukewarm hearts, then so be it by your choice.

My time is limited in being able to address you.

You cannot wonder why the Lord's judgement will be dealt in accordance to your actions.

It is your choice and the work of divine grace demands effort from you.

Peace, little children.

I bless you in the name of Jesus Christ, the LORD GOD.

Thank you for your necessary response to My call.

AD DEUM.

Our Lady's Message of February 23,1995
through Gianna Talone Sullivan

My dear little children, praise be Jesus!

Little ones, let the crucifix be your first source of help on days of misfortune and sufferings.

You will find comfort in your sufferings at the foot of the cross.

Gaze upon the crucifix with affectionate adoration.

You are redeemed through the sufferings of My Son and He will give to you the strength and courage He asks of you.

Little ones, in your suffering you are submerged into the abandonment of My Son and salvation results through His Mercy.

Do not seek consolation and strength from people, but embrace instead the foot of the cross when you are afflicted with misery.

Turn to your merciful Savior in your bitter suffering.

He will strengthen you and help you to endure all afflictions.

He will restore your peace, replace your weakness with courage, strengthen you in tranquility and change your sorrow to joy.

I love you, little ones, and I present your petitions to My Son.
Peace. Thank you for responding to My call.
AD DEUM.

(Our Lady blessed all the priests and lay people. She was
radiantly glowing (an aura of light which never left Her
was around Her.) Just before She left a light from heaven
beamed on Her head and She looked up, smiled and
blessed us, then left upward.)

Our Lady's Message of March 2,1995
through Gianna Talone Sullivan

My dear little children, praise be Jesus!
Little ones, Jesus loves you. He will take care of you.
You are His little children and you belong to Him.
During this Lenten season focus on My Son's Mercy.
His merciful Heart is for all sinners.
There you will find rest and security.
You are not alone, little children.
God is with you.
Invite the Holy Spirit to enlighten your mind, your soul and your
heart.
Do little sacrifices of love in honor of My Son's merciful Heart.
This is a time of mercy.
In all you do, remember Jesus' sufferings.
In this you will find consolation.
Ponder how the world treated your Savior and you will find strength
in your sufferings dealt from the world.
If your heart is heavy, contemplate how heavy was your Savior's
Heart who accepted persecution for love of you.
You are called to be like Him.
You are His little children.
If you are sorely afflicted, accept your suffering for the love of
Him.
No servant is greater than his master.
All who are close to heaven suffer as My Son.

God purifies you and chastises those He loves.
It is how you grow in humility and great virtues of love and charity.
I am with you little ones and I take your petitions to Jesus.
I bless you in His name. Peace.
Thank you for responding to My call.
AD DEUM.

Our Lady's Message of March 9,1995
through Gianna Talone Sullivan

My dear little children, praise be Jesus!
Little ones, I am your Mother of Joy because I bring to you "Life".
I bring you My Son, your Savior, Jesus.
He is Life.
I point the way to Him.
I watch and protect all children.
You, little ones, regardless of gender or age are called to be child-like.
I give to you the Child Jesus, pure and innocent.
He is Joy and it is My joy to present Him to you.
He is your Joy.
Do not destroy the gift of Joy by destroying the gift of Life.
Protect life in love and through prayer.
I am here to protect all life and no forces of evil can prevail over Me.
This place is the haven of life because it is center of My Immaculate Heart where all children seek refuge.
It will withstand all attacks from evil because I am here with My Child Jesus.
It is a center of refuge for all children.
Here they will find Joy, for I am your Mother of Joy and I present Jesus your Joy as a Child.
Jesus comes in the form of a child when He is filled with joy.
Little ones, this place is the only place in the history of My appearances that I have been allowed to come presenting the Child Jesus as the source of refuge for all children.

He humbles Himself in His Majesty to come with Me in the form
of a little child offering you the invitation of life and joy.
Come, little children, to Jesus. Come.
I bless you in His name.
Thank you for responding to My call. AD DEUM.

(It should be known that Our Lady comes in Scottsdale
under the title of Our Lady of Joy but not with the
Child Jesus. Scottsdale is called center of Jesus'
Divine Mercy. Emmitsburg is center of Our Lady's
Immaculate Heart, but She brings Child Jesus.)

Our Lady's Message of March 16, 1995
through Gianna Talone Sullivan

My dear little children, praise be Jesus!
Little ones turn to God for spiritual enlightenment so that you will
gain the knowledge needed to love.
You cannot love unless you have the knowledge of His love.
He is the Word.
The more you seek to know Him through His Word, the deeper
will be the scope of your love.
Little ones, do not keep your distance from God.
To love is to have faith.
The longer you keep your distance from God, the longer you will
suffer from lack of love.
For those who do not believe do not love. God is Love.
A lack of love is a lack of faith and a lack of conviction in seeking
clear knowledge of the truth.
Little ones, turn to God.
He will help you love as He is Love.
Ask Him to enlighten you with the gift of knowledge.
God loves you and desires to give the world peace.
You are all invited to open your hearts so that love and dignity can
be restored.

Peace cannot exist unless there is love.

I bless you, little children, in the name of Jesus,My Son.

Thank you for responding to My call.

AD DEUM.

Our Lady's Message of March 23, 1995
through Gianna Talone Sullivan

My dear little children, praise be Jesus!

Little ones, if you suffer affliction, persecution or opposition from the world, do not fear.

My Son lived a life filled with difficulty, outrage and persecution.

The world treated Him harshly and people who were ungrateful killed Him.

When My Son gives you His virtues, do not be surprised when they are met with opposition and you suffer the persecution and scoffing of the world.

You are suffering as My Son suffered, and it is evidence of a true virtue from God.

One true virtue will not destroy another. Be at peace.

No servant is greater than His master.

You serve God, and in Him your hopes and desires will be fulfilled.

Turn to Jesus, little ones. Tell Him your afflictions.

Ask Him to help you.

Be open and candid with Him.

He will fill you with a holy freedom and protect you.

Nothing unfolds in this world without God's permission.

You may not understand, little ones, but with time you will come to understand how everything is providential and serves God.

I bless you, little children, with the light of God's peace.

Be not afraid.

Move forward in the courage of God's love with confidence.

Thank you for responding to My call.

AD DEUM.

Our Lady's Message of March 30,1995
through Gianna Talone Sullivan

My dear little children, praise be Jesus!

Little ones do not be discouraged when at times you are afflicted with trials.

Jesus allows this to happen, but He then restores His tranquility in you.

This is how you are distinguished by Gods most intimate love.

You must desire to imitate Jesus and follow Him in His Passion.

By meditating on the Passion of My Son you will attain the summit of perfection of His love.

It is the bread of life, little ones, which starves the loves of worldly affections but gives wisdom to those who embrace the cross.

There are many people who desire to be distinguished in God's love and to be highly favored without imitating Jesus in His Passion.

They desire to be pardoned without penance.

Eternal rest is incompatible with not having labored for it through the imitation of Jesus.

How do you expect to go before God the Father and reign with Jesus if you do not accept to follow Him or imitate Him in His sacred Passion?

Bless Jesus, little ones, for His love for you and offering Himself for your salvation.

Embrace your cross with joy and tranquility of heart.

Seek to follow Him even in your sufferings.

I bless you, little ones, in the name of Jesus who has allowed Me to be here with you.

Thank you for responding to My call.

AD DEUM.

Our Lady's Message of April 6, 1995
through Gianna Talone Sullivan

My dear little children, praise be Jesus!

Little children, come to Jesus.

Jesus is the bridge to the Father.

No one can come to the Father except through Jesus.

The Father is loving and tender.

The Father is the Living Water of Grace.

Persevere in this mortal life and know that My Son is the means of Divine union with human nature.

He is your victory in the life of everlasting glory.

Persevere, for perseverance receives the crown of glory.

All you who thirst, come to the living waters.

Come, little children.

You must have thirst to receive the holy virtues which lead to the state of perfection of love.

You must desire to drink the water of everlasting grace in order to persevere.

If you do not thirst for the living waters, you will not be able to be a vessel of love.

I love you, little children, and invite you to the water of everlasting life.

I bless you in the name of Jesus who is the bridge to the Father for He has said "No one comes to the Father except by Me".

Come, little ones, come to Jesus.

All you who are thirsty, come to drink the water of everlasting grace. Peace.

Thank you for responding to My call.

AD DEUM.

Our Lady's Message of April 20,1995
through Gianna Talone Sullivan

My dear little children, praise be Jesus!

Little ones, I am a Mother of Mercy.

Be at peace, Jesus is with you.

I love you, little ones, and desire you to grow in the love and holiness of My Son.

Do not be hard on yourself because of your sinfulness.

Trust in God's mercy.

Reform your ways through purity, chastity, honesty, loving each other in charity, and through prayer.

111

God makes the truth of your sinfulness known because He loves you and desires you to come to Him.

But you must have mercy on yourself and forgive yourself so God can forgive you and make you whole in His love.

Always choose to live a life free from sin and to love as Jesus is Love.

Do not be sad, but rejoice in His mercy and know He has given you the grace to see yourself as you are in the light of hope that you will turn to Him and seek to be meek and humble of heart.

Remember, little children, you cannot have a pure heart unless you forgive, including your very self.

God loves you. I love you.

Be at peace. Move forward with courage and hope.

Pray, little children! Pray! Do not be slothful in your prayer.

Be on guard against the evil one and his deceiving ways.

Prayer is your protection against evilness and the way to grow in knowledge of the truth of the deception of sin.

Thank you, little ones, for responding to My call.

I bless you in His name. Peace. AD DEUM.

(Our Lady gave a special blessing on all priests.
She said they suffer tremendously. She prayed over
everyone and blessed everyone. She left upward
in the sign (shape) of a cross.)

Our Lady's Message of April 27,1995
through Gianna Talone Sullivan

My dear little children, praise be Jesus!

My little ones, I have bestowed upon you many blessings in the name of Jesus and have given you many proofs that I am your Mother.

I have been with you in times of trials and persecution giving you hope and encouraging you to be strong in the name of Jesus.

I have pointed the way to My Son.

Now I invite you to defend God's ways through love and prayer and to avoid violence at all costs. Jesus loves you.

He has never abandoned you. He is always with you.

Do not be afraid to take a risk for His cause.

Do not be reluctant in defending Him against those who insult Him.

Defend His interests and honor through love not violence.

Imitate His love for you .

Take every opportunity to win hearts of others to Him.

Glorify My Son through prayer and deeds of love. Practice devotions in His Honor.

Remember, little ones, that Satan wants to destroy all people and have none turn to Jesus.

Satan desires to destroy mankind through hatred.

My Son on your behalf lived a difficult life and accepted the contempt of the world and cruelty with which He was treated and all persecution for the salvation of the world.

He accepted all persecution for love of you.

Now I invite you to defend His ways and to glorify Him through love and prayer.

I invite you to be servants of God for victory and freedom.

Remove all obstacles, little children, which are preventing you to walk the path of God and to love as He loves.

Pray to the Holy Spirit to enlighten you with the truth of the vices of your flesh so that you can grow in purity and holiness.

Thank you, little ones, for responding to My call.

I take your petitions to Jesus.

Be little children and win glory for God through your little acts of love and great devotion to prayer.

 I bless you in His name. Peace.

AD DEUM.

Our Lady's Message of May 4,1995
through Gianna Talone Sullivan

My dear little children, praise be Jesus!

Little ones, I have given you many messages of hope, joy, love and inspiration so that you may love all people unconditionally because this is the center of My Immaculate Heart.

I have not cried tears of blood or given messages of devastation or chastisements to come because I desire the world to know that those who trust in My Immaculate Heart and the Sacred Heart of My Son can rest in Our peace and joy.

All are invited to seek refuge in Our two Hearts of love.

Come, all My children.

I invite you, My children, to live My messages of hope, joy and love so that all the world will know God's truth and see that at this center of My Immaculate Heart there can only be hope, joy, love and a safe refuge for all children.

My Immaculate Heart shall triumph, and the Two Hearts shall reign in glory of the Eternal Father's Truth.

My little children, live in peace, unity, harmony and love for one another.

Do not allow any bitterness or hatred or jealousy to overcome you.

Dive into My Immaculate Heart and the Sacred Heart of Jesus.

I bless you, little ones, in the name of Jesus.

Thank you for responding to My call.

Peace.

AD DEUM.

Our Lady's Message of May 11,1995
through Gianna Talone Sullivan

My dear little children, praise be Jesus!

Little ones, do not be hard on yourself when you find you have made mistakes or have failed in responding to God's love.

Be loving and merciful towards yourself, for God is Love and Mercy.

Only God is perfect, and only when you dwell with the angels in heaven will you be free from sin.

God loves you in your weakness and invites you to trust in Him so that you can grow in holiness and humility.

If you seek to love as God loves and to do His will, God can turn your human weakness into a strong pillar to house great graces and virtues.

But if you have repugnance for your weakness, avoiding God's mercy, you will weaken, and vices of self-pride and lack of patience will prevent God's pillar of graces to rest with you.

Only through God can love exist, little children, for God is Love.
Be kind and merciful on yourself in times of error for God is teaching you how to grow in His perfection of love.
But if people avoid God's mercy and love, love and mercy will cease to exist and the greatest enemy against man will be man.
Peace, little ones.
I take your petitions to Jesus.
Thank you for responding to My call.
AD DEUM.

Our Lady's Message of May 18, 1995
through Gianna Talone Sullivan

My dear little children, praise be Jesus!
Little ones, I am the Mother of God, the Mother of your Savior, and I am full of grace.
I invite you to follow the perfection of God's love through My example.
To be full of grace you must have an all consuming love for God.
You must be dedicated to Him so that all your desires are to please God at every moment.
Put aside all forms of self-interest which are not subdued by a pure desire to please God and cooperate with Him.
Devote yourself without reservations to God's Holy Will.
Little children, God is the power of all life.
He is the depth of all knowledge.
Everything on earth needs His support in order to be in existence.
If God for one moment withdrew His love and power from anything, it would cease to exist and vanish into the nothingness from which God created it.
Trust in God, little children.
Place your confidence in Him alone.
It is the way to preserving peace and purity of heart.
Trust in God, little children.
Consolations from this world are limited and imperfect.
Trusting in God brings the deepest form of security, freedom, consolation and wisdom.

Desire only what God desires for you.

He will only send you the things that are best for you and for your happiness.

I bless you, little children, in the name of Jesus, your Savior.

I take your petitions to His most Sacred Heart. Peace.

Thank you for responding to My call.AD DEUM.

Our Lady's Message of June 1,1995
through Gianna Talone Sullivan

My dear little children, praise be Jesus!

Little ones, trust yourself entirely to God and His Divine Providence.

Allow Him to do whatever is necessary in your life without being anxious.

Turn to Him lovingly and allow Him to provide you with everything in His time and in the way which is best for your happiness.

Utilize the great gifts of faith, hope and charity that God has graced you with.

Have faith in God.

There is nothing that escapes Him.

Nothing can happen without His Divine permission.

Trust that He will direct you, guide you and provide for all your needs.

Hope in God.

Little ones, excite in yourselves that all will turn out for your happiness and advantage in love.

Even in times of difficulties and misery do not despair, but make an act of hope.

In addition, make an act of charity by extending your arms to God and attaching yourselves to His Divine Providence.

God has infinite wisdom and all His ways are good.

He leads you to holiness and perfection of His love.

Trust yourselves entirely to His Divine Providence and give Him complete power over your lives.

Nothing happens without His permission.

Peace, little ones.
Thank you for responding to My call.
AD DEUM.

Our Lady's Message of June 8,1995
through Gianna Talone Sullivan

My dear little children, praise be Jesus!
Little children, the love of God is pure and simple.
I desire for all of you little children to offer all of yourselves un-
conditionally to God.
Give to Him everything.
Penetrate His Heart by giving your heart to Him.
Invite Him to be with you every day in everything you do.
Ask Him to be with you and to change your heart to follow His
way of love.
God will never mislead you.
Believe in the living God and trust in Him.
God will dwell in you.
But if you are mean to one another, you are not permitting Him to
dwell in you, for God is Love and can only love.
Allow God to help you by asking Him to be with you, to dwell in
you, to change you more and more every day until you are like
Him.
Be Jesus, little children, "ipse Christus".
You will find joy in all you do.
You will even find joy in suffering, self-denial and sorrow.
You are little children of God.
The life of Jesus will be fulfilled in you step by step if you invite
Him.
Do not delay, little children.
It is a wonderful joy to know you are a child of God and are close
to the Father.
Do not keep your distance.
Ask and you shall receive .
I bless you, little children, and take your petitions to God.
Peace. Thank you for responding to My call.
AD DEUM.

Our Lady's Message of June 15,1995
through Gianna Talone Sullivan

My dear little children, praise be Jesus!

Little children, God comes to bring peace, good news and life to all people.

He loves you.

Unite with one another in prayer despite your differences.

Offer yourselves to God in reparation for the sins against My Son's most Sacred Heart.

Be "little children" of God.

To be" little" is to avoid focusing on yourself but to focus on God and to be dependent and confident in His love.

True joy can be masked through the resistance of the intellect.

Be little joyful children and join with Me in prayer and in love in reparation for the many sins against the Sacred Heart of Jesus.

Pray for the conversion of all sinners and for peace in the world.

It is very important that you pray every day and take seriously My call.

Satan is strong and is trying to destroy love in the world through division, scandals and deception.

Be aware, little children, and know God comes to bring peace and life to all people.

I love all you little children and invite each one of you to offer yourself to God unconditionally and allow Him to do whatever He desires in you, accepting whatever He sends your way.

I bless you, little children, in the name of Jesus.

Thank you for responding to My call.

AD DEUM..

Our Lady's Message of June 22,1995
through Gianna Talone Sullivan

My dear little children, praise be Jesus!

It is important that you refrain from judging others.

Only God sees the true incentives of each person's heart.

Rather, have a genuine love for one another.

Do not avoid, be distant or indifferent toward one another.

Do not be afraid.

It is important to love all people and to be genuinely sincere in your kindness and behavior of affectionate manner.

You are invited to participate in the Divine life of Jesus and to live in His intimate union with the Father.

Focus on the way of Jesus not on the way that others live.

Do not judge, for you know very little.

Seek to serve in love all people for this is what God desires.

You cannot serve only those people you desire and serve God.

To serve God is to serve all people with a genuine love.

Little children, seek to remain little children of God.

Seek to live in His truth and His love by focusing on Jesus and trusting in Him instead of focusing on others and trusting in yourselves.

I love you, little children, and invite you to give all of yourself to God unconditionally through love and acceptance of others.

Peace.

Thank you for responding to My call.

Our Lady's Message of June 29,1995
through Gianna Talone Sullivan

My dear little children, praise be Jesus!

Little ones, God is abiding in love!

He allowed Himself to be humiliated and offered Himself up as a sacrificial love for you.

He desires you to be happy little children and to be free from the slavery of pride, misfortune, dissatisfaction and all elements of misery.

Turn to Jesus, little ones, and first seek to give Him what is rightly due, mainly your very self.

Before you begin your daily responsibilities first go before God and give to Him your heart and all that unfolds each day.

In fidelity to God fulfill your daily duties in His love and for love of Him.

Frustration develops when you attempt to accomplish something on your own merit without seeking God's grace.

Do all things by God, for God, with God and in God.

Holiness is a direct response to your fidelity and cooperation with God in fulfilling your daily responsibilities.

Be at peace in all you do knowing We are with you.

Accept God's will as it unfolds daily and be joyful little children.

Pray with all your heart, at all times, in all you do.

Accept your frailties with gentleness and trust that God's hand is upon you.

I love you, little ones, and bless you in the name of My Son Jesus.

Thank you for responding to My call.

Peace. AD DEUM.

(Our Lady blessed everyone with a special grace which flowed from Her hands, especially on two priests who are celebrating their ordination to the priesthood.)

Our Lady's Message of July 6,1995
through Gianna Talone Sullivan

My dear little children, praise be Jesus!

It is important, little children, to always place God at the center of your works.

God is Love and He graces you to serve in an affectionate loving manner.

God desires all people to be free of anxiety and sorrows of the world.

This entails prayer and trusting in Him.

All people have faults, but if you pray you will be able to serve in an affectionate manner filled with His love.

Trust that God will give you the grace to be patient as you would desire people to be patient with you.

Trusting in God may not do away with your difficulties but grace will help you to bear them and free you from all anxiety.

The walk of My Son encompasses many sacrifices and you are given the opportunity to expiate sin through them.

Place God at the center of your life and take comfort in the thought
that the cross you carry is with Jesus and for Jesus.
I bless you, little children, in the name of Jesus and take your peti-
tions to His most Sacred Heart.
Thank you for responding to My call.
AD DEUM.

Our Lady's Message of July 13,1995
through Gianna Talone Sullivan

My dear little children, praise be Jesus!
Live your life, little ones, in a way which pleases Jesus.
Follow His teachings of faith, patience, perseverance and love.
Remain faithful to what you have learned from Jesus.
There are people who have chosen to be wicked and those who do,
will go from bad to worse if they continue to deny the truth of
My Son's words of life.
Do not be self-centered, ungrateful, abusive, lovers of money, dis-
obedient to your parents, slanderous or indifferent to what is
good.
Learn to oppose these foolish ways and make progress through the
knowledge of God's love in faith.
Do not stop following the truth of God by following your own
desires.
Always follow Jesus.
He is the way, the truth and the life.
He is the only way for He is God.
Return to Him NOW for if you choose to deny the truth of His way
it will be difficult to hear His voice and respond to Him when
He calls you to His Feast.
Pray, little children, and be merciful, loving children.
Do not lift your head from the yoke of Jesus.
I bless you, little ones, in the name of Jesus.
Peace to you.
Thank you for responding to My call.
AD DEUM.

Our Lady's Message of July 27,1995
through Gianna Talone Sullivan

My dear little children, praise be Jesus!
I desire you to reflect upon the needs of the poor.
Love the poor and comfort them by making use of any abundance
 God has blessed you with to help them.
Open your hearts to the needs of the poor and give unconditionally
 in all areas.
Do not place value on earthly possessions.
Realize that earthly possessions can be deceitful and harmful to
 you if they are not used to acquire heavenly treasures.
Help the unfortunate little ones and give according to your means.
Imitate those who are compassionate and give to those who have
 little.
Do not imitate those who close their hearts to the needs of others.
Make your goal to imitate Jesus.
Though He was rich He became poor that all people would be en-
 riched by His poverty.
If you possess Jesus, little children, you are rich indeed!
Concentrate on acquiring the riches of His love and the treasures
 of heaven.
Reflect on all the attachments you currently embrace and you will
 see that you are attached even to the little things you possess.
I bless you, little ones, in the name of Jesus.
Thank you for responding to My call.
AD DEUM.

Our Lady's Message of August 10,1995
through Gianna Talone Sullivan

My dear little children, praise be Jesus!
Little ones, rejoice in Jesus.
All of you little children are very important for God's plan to be
 successful.
You are needed to insure that His love unveils everyday.
Do not feel that you are forgotten or forsaken.

God loves each and every one of you.

You cannot comprehend now the fullness of His love for you, but that day of revival shall come in the fullness of time and you will then comprehend His love for you.

Be strong little children and persevere with patience.

Do not seek the consolation of God but seek the God of consolation.

Pray, little ones, pray with all your hearts so that God can open them like a flower and mold you into His likeness.

Allow Him to make your hearts like His, all merciful and loving.

It is necessary that you all live in harmony and unity so that all the world can see that you are little children of God's love and not a stubborn, selfish people seeking self-gain or power.

The world must see that all who walk with God, live in God and are faithful to His way of love by loving and giving unconditionally to all people.

Every day God invites you to say "yes" to His love.

I love you, little ones, and bless you in the name of Jesus.

Thank you for responding to My call.

AD DEUM.

Our Lady's Message of August 17, 1995
through Gianna Talone Sullivan

My dear little children, praise be Jesus!

Little children, pray with all your hearts so that you will be able to respond to God's calling for peace and harmony.

Pray so that you will be able to see His goodness in all people and to genuinely love one another and respond to their needs with gentleness.

God loves you, little children, but there are great forces of evil trying to distract you and confuse you.

In order to remain focused it is necessary that you pray with all your hearts and practice living in simplicity.

Train your mind not to be engulfed by sweet enticements of materialism or overpowered by distracting words which overcloud your mind.

Push all distractions away when you pray.

Do not pay attention to thoughts which may enter your mind while you pray.

Focus only on God's love for you.

Be grateful for His goodness and the many gifts He has blessed you with.

Offer yourselves to God unconditionally in reparation of the many sins which offend Him.

Love one another and give in simpleness to the needs of others and to the needs of your own self.

I love you, little children, and call you to live in peace and harmony.

God must be first in your lives in order to respond to Him in faithfulness, love and obedience.

Offer yourselves to Him in reparation for all the offenses made against the Sacred Heart of Jesus.

Bless you, little children, in the name of Jesus.

Peace to you.

Thank you for responding to My call. AD DEUM.

Our Lady's Message of August 24, 1995
through Gianna Talone Sullivan

My dear little children, praise be Jesus!

If you love Jesus then imitate Jesus.

Do not only recite daily prayers in His honor but give to Him external signs of your devotion to Him.

Make His spirit of peace, love, charity, obedience, humility and self denial your own.

Adapt your heart to be in union with God by being pure and submissive to God's will.

Be generous in your love and zealous for God's interests with a reverent love for Him.

God loves you, little children, and desires you to live in a world of peace, unity, freedom and happiness.

Due to the lack of response from many people to love, pray and live in faith, these days are filled with confusion, anger, crime, pride, chaos and little love.

You need time to change, little children, and there are few who are utilizing this time of mercy by responding to God's call.

There are currently subtle evil forces in your midst which can only be recognized and fought victoriously through constant prayer, love and faith in God.

The apostasy of the Church is at hand, little children, and it is necessary that you return to God in faith, love and unity without delay, for days ahead will become increasingly difficult and only those who are steadfast in faith will be able to patiently endure the many hardships in peace of God's love.

I bless you, little children, and once again I tell you there is no time for fear, only time for change.

I am your Mother of Joy and I come to you inviting you to return to God.

He is Joy. In Him rests true freedom. Peace, little ones.

Thank you for responding to this call. AD DEUM.

Our Lady's Message of August 31,1995
through Gianna Talone Sullivan

My dear little children, praise be Jesus!

Littles ones, if you are steadfast in faith, Jesus will lovingly protect you in times of hardships with His cloak of mercy.

He is merciful and is seeking those who desire mercy.

He is looking for those who will plead for mercy and forgiveness for all people.

Pray, little children, and return to God in love and mercy.

The apostasy of the Church is at hand because of the many who have neglected the Holy mysteries and sacraments.

There are many priests who have not been reverent and pious in the Holy Sacrifice of the Mass.

Many have lost their dedication to God for their love of honor and pleasures.

Many people are neglecting prayer because their interests are above God's interests in their order of priority.

People are not willing to risk all for God because they are afraid about the things they cannot see.

This reluctance to surrender is an element of control due to lack of faith and trust in God.

There are many now who even question whether God exists.

The forces of evil have entered into the minds of many people because they have neglected prayer.

Through lack of prayer and merciless actions mankind is asking God to abandon it to itself.

Pray for mercy, little children, and desire love and forgiveness for all people.

I love you and bless you in the name of Jesus.

Be generous souls of love and mercy!

Thank you for responding to My call. AD DEUM.

Our Lady's Message of September 21,1995
through Gianna Talone Sullivan

My dear little children, praise be Jesus!

Little ones, Jesus invites you to His Sacred Heart.

He invites you to seek all that is good and to live in His merciful love.

There is great power in prayer.

Jesus relents in punishment when He sees people praying with a merciful love.

There has been great devastation already to this world from the hands of many people due to their lack of mercy and indifference to pray.

God does exist, little children.

Unity comes through prayer and merciful love towards one another.

It comes from living the Word of God.

Unity does not come from focusing on an energy force within yourself.

Love is not an emotion connected to an energy force which will save this world.

You are not God.

You are God's children, a people He created to reign with Him in joy and freedom.

If you turn away from God and refuse to believe in His existence you in turn will eliminate your own existence.

Jesus is Love.

Only God can save you and the world.

Jesus is meek and humble of heart.

Seek to be like Him.

Seek to live in Him.

Seek to live in humility instead of seeking other forces and inner energies which will deceive you to think you have power to be God- like.

True power comes in prayer and loving to serve God in littleness.

Prayer, love and mercy gain unity and peace.

God is the only way to peace.

Be aware, little ones.

There are many forces of evil and deceptions which can lead you astray from the truth if you are not focused only on God.

I urge all people to return to God before it is too late.

I desire to protect you as a loving Mother.

Return to God.

Return to His sacraments and remain faithful to His Word.

Thank you, little children, for responding to this call. AD DEUM.

Our Lady's Message of September 28,1995
through Gianna Talone Sullivan

My dear little children, praise be Jesus!

Love all people, little ones.

Rise above arguments and difficulties through prayer and deeds of love.

Have confidence in God's mercy and love.

If you are confident you will trust Him with a dependent surrendering love.

Accept God's love and strive to be gentle, meek and humble of heart.

You are all very special to God.

There are evil forces trying to make you feel inferior and tempt you with unworthy feelings.

The evil one would like to confuse you and cause division among you in the most trivial situations in order that you would not focus on God's mercy and love.

If division exists among the least important issues, how can peace exist on a larger scale?

God calls all of you to pray and to join in unity through mercy and forgiveness of one another.

Join together and avoid issues that might stimulate friction, anger and division.

Forgive one another and rise to God's merciful ways of love.

Pray with confidence, and trust His mercy and love will soothe all broken hearts.

Pray and trust peace will exist.

Challenge yourself to show actions of love and gentleness, and without fail continually focus on Jesus.

His love is for you. All your actions must be centered on God.

All your words and thoughts must be centered on God.

Do not be distracted by focusing on the offenses of others.

If you are consumed with the trivial issues, how can God entrust you with larger ones of mercy?

Do not focus on the actions of others.

Focus on your own actions and strive to always be loving.

Refrain from speaking ill of one another or causing division at all levels.

Work towards the finish line of God's love.

Pray and be merciful and strive to be like Jesus in order that you will be able to see Him face to face with a pure heart.

I bless you, little ones, in the name of Jesus who has permitted me to be here with you.

Receive His peace and joy.

Thank you for responding to My call.

Our Lady's Message of October 5, 1995
through Gianna Talone Sullivan

My dear little children, praise be Jesus!

Little ones, have confidence in God.

Come draw near. I will not reject you.

God loves you and welcomes you in His love.

I am the refuge of sinners and I intercede for all who return to God aware of their many weaknesses and who put their trust and hope in God.

Do not remain stubborn in your designs of life.

God desires to protect you and lead you to victory during these days where evil is corrupting much of the world.

Little children, God made you to love Him.

Love Him children, courageously and fervently.

Be ready and willing to lose every possession except His grace rather than to commit sin by accepting evil .

It is most necessary that you master your passions now and only love what God loves.

Abandon yourself to Jesus. Trust in His guidance.

God has blessed the path each person must take to be holy.

You cannot be sanctified if you attempt to choose to travel a different path. This path calls you to love.

Love separates you from everything.

It will separate you from wealth, social position and anxiety.

Love will strip your soul of its material cover and liberate you in God's freedom.

Love and give to one another out of the affection of your heart not out of obligation or duty. Love has no measures.

I bless you, little children, and desire you to love as God loves.

He has unfathomable graces of mercy and love to give for all who will allow Him. Walk in the ways of God, little ones.

Do not continue to travel in the ways of your own designs.

Live the word of God and remain faithful to it.

Thank you for responding to My call. AD DEUM.

Our Lady's Message of October 12,1995
through Gianna Talone Sullivan

My dear little children, praise be Jesus!

God loves you and has blessed you abundantly.

Love Him with your whole heart.

He desires for you to seek Him in all you do with an affectionate heart.

Find delight in seeking Jesus and thinking of Him.

Do everything for Him so that the Kingdom of God will dwell within you.

Take time to spend with Jesus alone in prayer so that He may fill you with more graces.

There are few people who are at spiritual peace and joy because there are few people who will spend time alone with Jesus in prayer.

Do not be divided interiorly between distractions and useless affections and thoughts.

Dwell on Jesus, for only He alone will fill you with peace.

He alone occupies the thoughts and affections of an interior person.

Master all external affairs with an interior peace of heart.

Allow inner peace governed by God to rule over all external passions and situations.

Live every breath for Jesus.

Consecrate your entire being to God and entrust yourself to His care.

Direct all your actions, duties, intentions, affections and thoughts to Jesus.

Contemplate His love and the things that are in heaven.

You will live in peace and joy and master all degrees of passion with patience in His love.

I love you, little ones, and bless you in His name.

Thank you for responding to My call. AD DEUM.

Our Lady's Message of October 19 ,1995
through Gianna Talone Sullivan

My dear little children, praise be Jesus!

My little ones, pray with all your hearts for the Goodness of God is great indeed.

Overlook the failings of others and strive to be merciful and loving.

See the Goodness of God in each person.

If you desire to see through the eyes of Jesus, you cannot be righteous but all merciful and loving.

In order to see someone as Jesus sees, you must focus on God's Goodness in the person.

You must overlook the human weakness and sinfulness of the person and ponder how, through mercy, good surfaces in the end by means of love.

Humans are weak and sinful but that does not mean that every human cannot obtain everlasting life.

It does not mean that sinners cannot change and become God's instruments of peace.

Jesus did not die in vain. He is your Jesus of Hope.

Be merciful to all people and see God's Goodness in all people.

Mercy is not judgmental.

It is seeing others with the eyes of Jesus.

Do not be disrespectful but presume good in all people.

This applies also in receiving the graciousness of others, not only in giving.

I love you, little children, through the eyes of Jesus.

Please love others through His eyes.

I bless you in the name of Jesus.

Thank you for responding to My call. AD DEUM.

Our Lady's Message of October 26, 1995
through Gianna Talone Sullivan

My dear little ones, praise be Jesus!

Little children, the more you love, the more pleasure you will find in Jesus.

Love one another despite your differences and do not see yourself as favored and righteous in God's eyes.

Love each person and see how favored and righteous each person is through the eyes of Jesus.

If you select who you love, then you distance yourself from God and the less pleasure you will find in Jesus.

Jesus unites all the perfections of grace in Himself and brings you to Himself in this perfection of grace as you love.

My greatest treasure was in loving Jesus which surpassed all the riches of wealth the world could ever provide.

Love one another and receive the great treasure of Jesus Himself.
I love you, little children, and take your petitions to My Son.
Peace to you.
Thank you for responding to My Call. AD DEUM.

Our Lady's Message of November 2,1995
through Gianna Talone Sullivan

My dear little children, praise be Jesus!
God loves you.
Every moment you give to Him is filled with great delight and
triumph towards My Immaculate Heart.
God desires you to love Him beyond the depths of the sea.
He desires you to give yourself unconditionally to Him.
He blesses you and loves you.
He is not asking you to live extraordinary lives.
He desires you as you are in the ordinary ways of life.
There is much greed today because there are many people trying to
outdo others.
God is looking for the simple.
In simpleness you become extraordinary in the eyes of God.
There is much anger, crime, jealousy and hate towards one another
because of the lack of genuine love.
Give more of yourselves to God so that He can grace you and give
more to you.
Strive to be hospitable and genuinely loving so that the world will
see the joy of Jesus in your eyes here at this center of My Im-
maculate Heart.
All are called to be filled with joy.
To be filled with joy you must be filled with Jesus' love.
Be patient with all who come here, for God will grace you more
abundantly.
Do not contradict your actions of love by being quick to speak ill
of others.
Be true children of God by living actions of generosity and loving
kindness.
Your speech must reflect the love of God.

Be careful not to blame others, criticize or judge.
Words and behavior as such contradict love and prevent you from
being a child of God.
I love you, little ones, and desire all who come here to see the love
and joy of Jesus in your eyes. Peace, little ones.
Thank you for responding to My call. AD DEUM.

Our Lady's Message of November 9, 1995
through Gianna Talone Sullivan

My dear little children, praise be Jesus!
Little ones, hold on to Jesus in every trial, anguish or temptation.
Turn to Him. Have recourse to Him.
If you are given more crosses to bear, there are more graces which
God has planned for you.
He loves you and will not give you more than you can handle.
Unite your suffering to Jesus and offer in love all up to Him.
The sweetness of your sacrifice in love and self-abandonment con-
quers forces of evil.
I desire all of you little children to open your hearts to receive the
peace and comfort of Jesus.
Accept with patient resignation your crosses in life and turn to
Jesus and have recourse to Him.
Graces will flow abuntantly, and anguish will turn to tranquility,
and the peace and comfort of Jesus will result in your heart.
I desire for all who come here to know of the joy of Jesus.
I desire all who come here to receive hope and strength.
My Immaculate Heart is a refuge for all people.
All are welcomed.
You little children are invited to join together in unity to share My
love and joy in Jesus with all who come here.
Do not lose peace of heart when trials or discomforts befall you.
Do not lose hope but rejoice in Jesus because His plan for you is
great.
Have recourse to Him because in Him rests true peace and tran-
quility.
I love you, little children, and bless you in the name of Jesus.
Thank you for responding to My call. AD DEUM.

Our Lady's Message of November 16,1995
through Gianna Talone Sullivan

My dear little children, praise be Jesus!

Little ones, focus on Jesus your Savior.

Find your joy in Him above all created things.

In Jesus will you find an all satisfying love.

Find joy in Jesus above all enjoyments, comforts, health, glory, power and above all knowledge.

Jesus made you for Himself and He alone is full of consolation.

If you experience temptations and struggles of life turn to Jesus.

He will help you overcome these annoyances.

You will never be free from temptations in this life because there may be various circumstances, things and even people who may appeal to your weakness.

Keep your focus on Jesus, and by humility and patience you will become strong against the strains of this life and the spiritual enemies of your soul.

Correct what you can with a loving action and bear patiently the things which cannot be remedied.

I love you, little children, and desire you to be filled with joy and that your joy may be complete in Jesus.

I bless you and take your petitions to God your Creator.

Peace, little ones.

Thank you for responding to My call.

AD DEUM.

Our Lady's Message of November 30,1995
through Gianna Talone Sullivan

My dear little children, I come to you with the joy of Jesus your Savior.

Praise be Jesus!

This season draws close to every human's heart the joy of love in several forms.

Joy centered on Jesus and His mystical life shall bring forth interior peace and self satisfaction.

Reflect on the infant Jesus and wait in anticipation for His joyous coming, the most marvelous time of the year for all of humankind.

Ponder His goodness and holy indifference which allowed Him to rise to the heights of humility.

The joy of a mother surpasses all ailments and it is My joy to bring you to Him.

It is My joy for I am your Mother.

Strive to be little children who desire to guard His Word through faithfulness, love and humility by surrendering to Divine Providence.

Your fidelity to God, little ones, is the bond to unity and bridge to life.

It is not Jesus' desire that any one person miss the bridge of life and the waters from which graces flow.

He desires all to live in purity and integrity.

I bless you, little ones, in His love. I take your petitions to Him.

Blessed be His Holy Name!

Thank you for responding to My call. AD DEUM.

(Our Lady wants all to know She desires to be known under the title of Our Lady of Emmitsburg.)

Our Lady's Message of December 7,1995
through Gianna Talone Sullivan

My dear little children, praise be Jesus!

My little ones, in this world you walk blindly submitting to the demands of its customs; yet when it comes to submitting to Jesus and pleasing Him in obedience, you find it difficult.

Trust and confidence is what is needed.

God is with you in your trials.

He strengthens you.

Give yourself to God without seeking compensation.

Do not be concerned if you suffer without consolation because your love is becoming purer.

All those who follow Jesus have their cross and will end in the same fate as He.

The world may scorn against deeds, duties and practices you accomplish in hiddenness.

They may mock you because you do not make evident your virtues or win their honor or esteem.

Do not be discouraged, little ones, but be strong.

Seek God's approval only.

Remember this world is passing away but God's love never passes away.

May the Lord's glory inspire you to continue on in your duties to serve with love and generosity.

The honor you seek should not be from man.

Those who walk in this world's certainty are not walking in the certainty of God's truth.

Those who strive to live in humility may be seen through the eyes of the world as disrespectful, unkind and merciless.

Mocking may even exist within your Christian community.

What is needed is love, little children.

What is needed is selflessness, unity and hospitality.

The way of the Lord will contradict the way of this world in many facets of your life. Be patient and give yourself to God..

Do not be selfish by looking to your needs but look to the endpoint of God's reign and glory.

I bless you, little ones, and love you with the love of a mother.

Come to Jesus, your Emmanuel, and be at peace.

I take your petitions to Him.

Thank you for responding to My call. AD DEUM.

Our Lady's Message of December 14,1995
through Gianna Talone Sullivan

My dear little children, praise be Jesus!

Each day, little ones, God graces you with His merciful love.

He awaits your love and waits for you to turn to Him in the secrecy of your hearts

He desires for you to embrace His mercy.

Little children, God promises to protect those who trust in Him.

Give Him all your cares because He cares for you.

He will help you however difficult your situation.

Hope in him.

God will give you peace and tranquillity even if at times it seems He has abandoned you.

God will not forget you.

Many times God may not liberate you in your afflictions or answer your prayers as you desire.

This does not mean God has abandoned you. His plans are no less wondrous.

His plans are perfect, and in affliction His blessings are greater to those who trust and hope in Him.

Please correspond to the grace God gives you.

It may not alleviate your afflictions but will help you to bear them.

Ask God, little ones, to help you profit from your burdens and turn to Him for His mercy.

You will gain more virtues.

I love you, little ones, and bless you in the name of Jesus.

I bless you with His peace.

Thank you for responding to My call. AD DEUM.

Our Lady's Message of December 21,1995
through Gianna Talone Sullivan

My dear little children, praise be Jesus!

The time of arrival is drawing near when Jesus, your Savior, will calm every fear and wipe every tear.

Rejoice, oh highly favored ones of God, that God's mercy is infinite and His love all abounding in truth.

This season is one of peace for all who carry the truth of love in their hearts.

Love cures every ailment and is the healing balm to hatred.

Love strengthens the soul and can cure any illness.

Love lives by the will of God with fortitude and perseverance as the virtues to holiness.

You can love, little ones.

You can love all people even though you may not receive love in return.

Do not fight evil with evil.

Do not fight back with vengeance and hatred in order for justice to prevail.

The justice of God does not consist of punishment as a result of anger and hatred.

Justice consists of mercy and love.

Seek to live only for God and by God's way, little ones.

Do not be fearful, but be at peace for God does exist and you are not forgotten.

Do not focus on yourself, your short comings, or how you can do better.

Focus on the love of God in others.

I bless you, little ones, on this holy occasion of preparation for the coming of your Emmanuel. Let us join together in love.

Let us live together in the silence of His peace.

May the sacredness of His love silence your anxieties and give you hope for tomorrow.

Peace, little ones.

Peace to you in the name of your Savior, Jesus. AD DEUM.

Our Lady's Message of January 4, 1996
through Gianna Talone Sullivan

My dear little children, praise be Jesus!

Little ones, reflect on God's love for you and see how all things are orchestrated to fulfill His most perfect plan.

If you seek His will and not your own, you will be satisfied in this time period of your life where God has placed you.

God blesses each person according to the plan He has destined for that person.

He graces each person in order to fulfill each responsibility.

This is how you grow in holiness and God blesses you as you travel His path.

Whatever circumstance or state of mood you find yourself, remember you are safest when you trust in God and remain faithful to Him.

Holiness is not related to place, state of emotion or occupation.

It is related to yourself.

Holiness is not serving God as you would like, but as He desires.

You can change your current situation by changing your occupation or vocation, but your flaws will follow you wherever you
go unless you change yourself.

Give all of yourself to God and allow Him to purify you.

Trust He has placed you where He desires you to be in order to
grow in holiness.

Trust He has a plan for you.

I love you, little ones, and take your petitions to God.

Receive His peace.

Thank you for responding to My call. AD DEUM.

Our Lady's Message of January 25, 1996
through Gianna Talone Sullivan

My dear little children, praise be Jesus!

The delight of a true friendship is when there is a holy friendship.

Little children, use prudence in your selection of friends.

Seek those whom you know you can rely on by the virtues of their
religious spirit.

Many friendships may seem to be sincere in the beginning but fade
because faults are the only common bond.

Be aware, little children, of what constitutes a true friendship.

Look to choose friends of virtue.

Seek those who live by examples of love.

Seek those who comfort, guide and counsel.

Seek those who live a life of SOLID PRAYER and those whose
tongues fall silent to evil speech and indecent gossip.

It is far better to be quiet and live a life of solitude than to partake
in worldly humor exposing yourself to the danger of sin.

It is not how cordial or friendly you are which connotes a sincere
friendship.

A life of prayer, honesty, commitment, and actions of love are proof
to a virtuous and long lasting friendship.

Love virtue itself by loving Jesus.

Little ones, measure friendship with prudence by looking for the
virtues of solid prayer.

You will find that the fruits of solid prayer have no special regard for any person in particular.

All are friends to that person.

A person of prayer grows in practical goodness and the warmth of his love reaches out to all people, friend, enemy or stranger.

I bless you, little ones, and take your petitions to My Son, who has allowed me to be with you in a very special way.

Thank you for responding to My call.

AD DEUM.

Our Lady's Message of February 1, 1996
through Gianna Talone Sullivan

My dear little children, praise be Jesus!

Little ones, Jesus died to save all people who repent of their sins and seek the mercy of God.

Your primary focus in this life should be centered on God.

Do not dwell on any circumstance in particular, or on any person, friend, stranger or even enemy.

Focus on God alone and He will give you the grace to grow in practical goodness and love.

In this way all people will be equally dear to you for the warmth of your love will extend out to all people whether they be friend, stranger or enemy.

Do not focus on your prestige, material goods, success or self-image, for they will have no value when you go before the throne of God and see Him face to face.

It is the state of your soul that is of an urgent matter and needs to be nurtured.

In this life only love can touch God, as He is Love, not your material goods, knowledge or status.

This is why I urge you, little ones, to work with fervent love on rescuing your own souls from the jaws of sin.

Ask God to purify you from the effects of your own personal sins.

Do not give up or become anxious about failing.

God will have recourse to you because He wants you to realize that He is all merciful and almighty.

Little children, as your Savior was presented in the temple to God, I present you to Him this night.

I bless you in His name and shed My merciful love on you as your Mother.

Peace to you.

Thank you for responding to My call. AD DEUM.

Our Lady's Message of February 8,1996
through Gianna Talone Sullivan

My dear little children, praise be Jesus!

Little children, examine what comes between you and Jesus.

There are many distractions you concentrate on intead of focusing your attention on Jesus.

Many times you go before My Son, or begin to think about Him, and you find yourself thinking of other things.

Distractions are thoughts, desires and feelings which captivate your attention.

If you allow your imagination to wander, you will be bound by the grip of distractions.

These distractions can be diminished by eliminating many aspects in your life without neglecting your duties and responsibilities.

As you attend to various people and duties throughout your day restrain the amount of attention that is given to only what is necessary.

This will allow you to be closer to My Son by allowing you to concentrate your attention on Him.

This does not mean that you are to love less.

This means to give all your love and attention to each person and circumstance as is necessary and to make a determined effort on concentrating on My Son.

Do not give your attention to what seems unnecessary.

Examine now how many things in your life that can be eliminated without neglecting your responsibilities and daily duties.

I love you, little ones, and take your petitions to My Son who loves you.

Peace to you, little ones.

Thank you for responding to My call. AD DEUM.

Our Lady's Message of February 15,1996
through Gianna Talone Sullivan

My dear little children, praise be Jesus!
Little ones, be generous with one another in the Spirit of Love.
Be generous when God asks anything of you.
Do not love only when it suits your interests for to serve God is to serve Him without conditions and with a sincere heart.
Be willing to give all of yourself to every wish from My Son.
Jesus loves you and has given to you all that is good.
Your generosity to My Son is proof of your love for Him.
Even in times of difficulty, be willing to give to My Son.
Do not lose heart but have hope in Him.
A true lover loves whether there is pain or comfort.
Stand firm in your love during times of conflict and afflictions, tribulations or persecutions.
God is never outdone in generosity, and He infinitely loves you.
But He asks those who desire to love, to love, persevere and be generous in all circumstances.
Love one another and submit to God's wishes with an unconditional heart.
God wants all your love.
Always give to Him whatever He asks and do whatever He tells you to do, without worrying whether it is too much.
The more you give the greater favors and rewards you will receive for He is preparing you to do great works for His glory.
I love you, little ones, and bless you in His name.
Peace to you.
Thank you for responding to My call. AD DEUM.

Our Lady's Message of February 22, 1996
through Gianna Talone Sullivan

My dear little children, praise be Jesus!
During this season take time to reflect on how you can be more merciful, loving and kind.
Little offerings to God are graciously received.
In times of difficulty, acts of patience, self composure and prayer

will help you rise above whatever ailment stresses you.

Offer each sacrifice up to God with love.

Persevere as each circumstance arises each day.

Be patient with yourself and love yourself knowing that this too shall pass.

There is nothing in this world that lasts forever but in the next all remains.

There is joy, happiness and peace in eternal life.

Pray for tranquility of heart.

God is with you. God knows you and will help you.

There is a great deal of pain which afflicts many people in different forms, for this is the way of the present world.

Yet those who hope in the joy of Jesus will rise to live in His joy.

Jesus will never abandon you. Be at peace knowing He is with you.

Calm your anxieties through love and acceptance of yourself and meet each frustrating circumstance with an open heart.

See each element of your life's experience as an opportunity to grow in love and humility. You will master your difficulties through a resigned and contrite heart.

I love you, little children, and desire you to grow in love and live in unity.

It is important that each of you work at striving to be patient and loving with yourself and each other.

God graciously receives these little offerings of sacrifice and He will grace you in your efforts. Only God can grace you to grow in love and is pleased with your sincere effort.

I bless you, little ones, and take your petitions to Him who has sent Me to you.

Thank your for responding to My call. Thank you for responding to His call. AD DEUM.

Our Lady's Message of February 29, 1996
through Giannna Talone Sullivan

My dear little children, praise be Jesus!

Little ones, offer to God a blind awareness of your own being.

This will enrich your interior life with a loving and delicate spiritual knowledge.

This will allow you to offer God a precious gift.

It unites yourself to God continually in the midst of your daily activities.

Absorb yourself in His love and you will be secure, gentle and fearless.

You will rest quietly in the loving contemplation of God and be wonderfully nourished.

You will gain strength and forget the concerns of the flesh.

You will grow in loving confidence of His truth and you will realize how much God loves you as you are in your weakness.

Each day you have the opportunity to grow in His love.

Each opportunity to love is unique in itself and passes by once.

Be inspired by this wisdom and glorious gift of love.

Love yourself as you are in your weakness.

Go about your daily activities continually offering to God your entire being, and share an outward expression of love to others.

You will be made perfect both interiorly and exteriorly through His grace.

A blind offering of yourself unites you to God and allows you to fulfill the designs of His plans for you.

I bless you, little ones, with His peace.

I take your petitions to the Father.

Thank you for responding to My call. AD DEUM.

(Our lady prayed a very long time with us and blessed everyone.)

PART III

Messages from Our Lord and Our Lady Given through the Our Lady's Prayer Group (St. Maria Goretti's Roman Catholic Church, Scottsdale, AZ)

February 1993 - March 1996

February 18, 1993
Message from Our Lady

My dear little children, I love you and come always in the name of my Son. Praise be Jesus. Look to Him, my little ones. It is so important that you always look first to my Son to grace you. He is the one who loves you to grace you with His virtues. My little ones, His way may not initially be your way but, if you surrender to Him and trust Him, then you will be able to trust others. First look to God. Procure your relationship with God first; and then you will have the blessings to love unconditionally, and to trust one another. I present to you my Son. Receive Him. Hope in Him and always look to Him for guidance in the midst of your confusion. I bless you, my little ones, in the name of my Son. Thank you, my little ones, for responding to my call.

March 4, 1993
Message from Our Lady

My dear little children, praise be Jesus! My little ones, remember that you belong to Jesus and, if you plunge yourselves into His heart, you will be awakened to a renewed way of living. Put aside your distractions and know you belong to Him. Do not be frustrated or discouraged. No matter what happens, you have my Son. Only in my Son can you live in peace and in love during these difficult times. Be at peace and joy-filled little children knowing He is here with you and will never leave you because you belong to Him. Bless you, my little ones, and thank you for responding to my call.

March 11, 1993
Message from Our Lady

My dear children, I come to bring tidings of peace. I am your mother who loves you. My Son loves you, my little ones. Please focus on Him. Take the time to be with my Son in His Eucharistic presence. He enthusiastically awaits you. Look to Him for acceptance and understanding before looking to one another in times of struggle. My little ones, only Jesus has the power, wisdom and knowledge to help you. He will bless you with abundant graces if you simply surrender and love Him.

My dear, dear children, I ask you again to put aside your trivial misunderstandings which are preventing you from focusing on my Son. Make straight your way of love through my Son. Only He can lead you in the true way of love. Thank you for responding to my call.

March 18, 1993
Message from Our Lady

My dear children, I am your mother who comes to be with you this night. I wrap you in my mantle of love. Children, your journey to my Son is by faith, not by sight. Continue to walk in your blindness, but know my Son and I are here with you walking every step. My Son is leading you, my little ones! Be patient in your blindness. Be patient in your trials. LOVE! My dear ones, pray with all your hearts. I love you! Peace to you!

March 18, 1993
Message from our Lord

My dear ones, I come this night to remind you of how much My Father loves you. He sends Me this night to ask again for your faithfulness. My dear ones, you are faithful! I give you My strength this night to continue on your faithful journey back to My Father. You do listen to My voice. How thankful I am to you! You are at last listening to Me! As you listen, I will continue to speak to each of you and to all of you. Listen with your whole being. Through your faithfulness I will be able to touch many. Please continue to be faithful no matter what anyone else says or does. Listen to Me. Come to Me and I will give you rest, and strength, and peace. I bless you, my faithful ones. I love you!

March 25, 1993
Message from Our Lord

My dear ones, this night I come to remind you of what a gift I have given you in My mother. She is the sign — the sign of trust, the sign of obedience, the sign of humility. She is the sign of all times reminding everyone of who God is! My dear ones, I ask you to cherish her, to cherish her presence with you. She loves you as do I. Follow her humility, follow her obedience, follow her trust, and she will lead you back to Me. Honor her as I honor her, and know that I love her as she loves Me. This night, in her honor, I bless you with My mercy, My peace!

April 1, 1993
Message from Our Lady

My dear little children, I am your mother, so full of grace. I tell you this night grace is being poured out to all my children. I ask you at this time to allow yourself to walk in a silent journey with my Jesus. Allow Him to bring you so close to His heart. Offer to Him all your joys and all your sufferings as you walk silently with my beloved Jesus. I love you, my little ones, and I bless you.

April 1, 1993
Message from Our Lord

My dear ones, again this night I come to ask that you trust in Me and in the will of My Father Who has sent Me. My dear ones, so much you try to understand My will and the will of My Father. It would be better if you would try as hard to trust in Me. The closer you come the more it seems you become distracted trying to understand. If you do not trust you will never understand. My dear ones, what My Father has for you is beyond anything you could ever imagine. Please believe Me when I say you need to trust in God. I love you. Trust in God. Trust this night in what I say to you.

April 22, 1993
Message from Our Lord

My dear ones, I, your Risen Lord, am here this night to remind you again that I am with you; that I walk with you; that I live in My Spirit within you; that you are never alone or away from Me. My dear ones, I give you My life. I call you this night to accept the love and the mercy and the compassion that God, My Father, and your Father, offers you through Me.

I encourage you — listen to Our Holy Spirit speaking to your heart. Take courage, be strong! Even in your weakness your strength is the strength that I give you. Stand in My light and be that light, My light to those around you. Live My truth and My joy, and allow My peace to flow through you to others. I bless you this night with My healing mercy. Rejoice, my dear ones, for because of My Father's love I have conquered even death, not only for Myself but for you. I love you. My peace is with you.

May 6, 1993
Message from Our Lord

My dear ones, this night I invite you agai to come to Me and to open your hearts so that I may come to you. I ask you to bring to Me each day all of those things that are part of your suffering and part of your joy. Offer them to Me so that I may take them to the Father, your Father and My Father. Give them to Me so that you do not have to carry them alone. My dear ones, you tire yourselves! Allow Me to strengthen you and to renew you, but for this you must come to Me. I love you and I wish to heal you, and forgive you, and strengthen you. Know that My Father has sent Me to be with you — and I am! This night I bless you again with My mercy and My peace.

May 13, 1993
Message from Our Lady

My dear little children, praise be Jesus! My dear ones, the Mass is the greatest prayer. Humble yourselves before my Son in the Mass and He will make you perfect. He will give to you all which you need to make you righteous in Him. My little ones, Satan is trying to destroy families and is very aggressive now against the youth. Pray, Pray, Pray! He knows his time is soon over and he is trying desperately to gather all and destroy your happiness. Pray and love one another. Love, please! I implore you to conversion and prayer now. I need your prayers. My Son is merciful. He is MERCY. He is LOVE. Bless you, my little ones. I take your petitions to my Son. Come, my little ones. Please return back to my Son through the sacraments and pray for the youth. Thank you for responding to my call.

May 13, 1993
Message from Our Lord

My dear ones, I come to you this night to tell you once again that I give you, I offer you, My mercy. As you accept My mercy, you will experience living in the love of My Father with Me. I offer you also this night the gift of My joy, the joy that is also My mother's joy. There is only one way to live in this joy that I offer, the joy in which My mother lives, and it is to keep the commandments of My Father as My mother did, as I did. This is truly, my dear ones, the source of joy. You know this already. It is truly simple, but I know also it is very difficult. I give you then, because of this difficulty, My strength this night to overcome the evil one, the strength of My Spirit which banishes him forever. Accept this tonight and, through this strength, My mercy will flow, My love will be in your heart and you will be surrounded in joy. Know that I am with you always. There is nothing to fear; and My mother will lead you, if you allow her, to Me, and together she and I will present you to God Our Father. I love you! I LOVE YOU!

May 20, 1993
Message from Our Lady

My dear children, praise be Jesus. My dear little ones, pray that you will be intimate with Jesus with a deep living faith that will bring you into His sweetness of love which surpasses all knowledge. My Son loves you, my children, and wishes for you to love one another unconditionally, without reservations and without judgment. Please, my little ones, love and allow yourself to be loved. Do not allow Satan to disrupt your focus. Please, I need you and I need you to look beyond to His love, removing yourselves from your own self-interests. He will give you abundant graces and heal your wounds with His tender love. Bless you, my little ones, for responding to my call.

May 20, 1993
Message from Our Lord

My dear ones, as Heaven and earth celebrate this feast of My ascension into Heaven, I am with you this night to remind you that I am always with you, that I do keep my promise, that I am here. My dear ones, just as My disciples did not understand what I said to them, I see you also not understanding. I know, My dear ones, it is so very difficult for you to trust in what I say because, for you, My will seems to take such a long time. My dear ones, look upon My disciples and see how I fulfilled what I said to them. I gave them My spirit, Our Spirit, the Spirit of My Father and Me, the same Spirit We have given to you. Use this day as an encouragement to you to be faithful and to trust in Me. I am with you now, and always and I am coming again. I give you this night the gift of My hope and My perseverance. I love you! I love you! Endure!

May 27, 1993
Message from Our Lady

My dear little children. Praise be Jesus. My little ones, the true experience is that of your faith. It is given to you from God. Always look to His goodness and live His word. Read the scriptures; study them, and the Holy Spirit will guide you in truth. Never fear because Jesus is your Saviour. But please pray and look to Jesus so He can cleanse you, teach you, guide you and protect you. God awaits your love patiently. Give all of your hearts in prayer to Him. God is living and is everywhere because of His creation of the world. Be at peace, my little children, and prepare in reconciliation and prayer for Pentecost. I bless you in Jesus. Thank you for responding to my call.

May 27, 1993
Message from Our Lord

My dear ones, I, your Saviour, your Jesus of Mercy, am with you. I come this night to encourage you no matter what the odds or barrier, to live My truth, to speak My truth. Before you can live or speak that truth which is Mine, you need to listen to Me, your Lord, who speaks continually to your heart. Come to Me. Come away with Me and listen. Be refreshed with My truth. Be energized with My very life. I have given you Our Spirit, the Holy Spirit of God; and I, your Lord, bless you this night with My peace. Be joyful, My little ones, as you live and speak the truth for the truth will not only vindicate you but will set you free. Remember I am always with you, always with you!

June 3, 1993
Message from Our Lady

My dear little children, praise be Jesus. My little ones, Jesus has graced you abundantly in ways you do not even recognize. Always be grateful and continue to seek Him in His love and tenderness. There are many things that you may not understand and may not even know the changes that my Son is doing in you. Be assured that by trusting in Him that there are many beautiful changes and fruits surfacing in your lives. My little ones, I ask you for unconditional trust and surrender, love and forgiveness and patience. Have hope, my little ones. God is with you. We are here for you because of love for you. Pray little ones. Pray fervently. I bless you in the name of my Jesus of Mercy. Peace to you. Love one another in His peace. Thank you for responding to my call.

June 3, 1993
Message from Our Lord

My dear ones, I come in love this night to you to bless those of you who are living the sacred covenant and sacrament of marriage. Know, my dear ones who My Father has called to live this life, that I am with you. Take courage and be strengthened by My love this night. Know that in living the sacrament, I am with you; in your patient endurance of trials, I am with you; in the joy of each other and of your family, I am with you. Know that you are a sign of God's hope for this world. Take courage, My dear ones, for a call to live this life of selfless love that nothing goes unnoticed by My Father. Nothing is so small of your self-sacrifice that is not worth much in the Kingdom of My Father. I thank you this night for responding in love to this call. I bless each of you and your families. Know that I am always with you.

June 10, 1993
Message from Our Lady

My dear little children, praise be Jesus. My little ones, know that not all relationships are easy to deal with. But if Jesus is in your heart there will be love. My Son has so many graces which He wishes to give to you and as you surrender in trust daily, He is able to give to you every source of strength and grace needed to procure a healthy and happy relationship. Be at peace in your daily walk, my little ones, as you give unconditionally to Jesus. He is with you and He will make every fruit blossom in every situation which you think is impossible. Nothing is impossible with God. Your focus, however, must always be on Jesus and your happiness and growth of holiness in Him. I bless you, my little ones, and thank you for responding to my call of patience in relationships with love being your source of light and peace.

June 10, 1993
Message from Our Lord

My dear ones, I come to you this night to remind you of the gift of freedom that you have been given through Our Holy Spirit. This freedom, My dear ones, freedom in the Lord is a gift truly which sets your spirit free. This freedom comes from obedience to My Father and to yours. My dear ones, I know how difficult it is sometimes to be obedient when this world in which you live is so disobedient to My Father and to yours. But know that as you are obedient you will experience more of the freedom of God. I love you, My dear ones. I encourage you in your obedience; and I offer My mother and Myself as your examples of obedience. This obedience will lead you through suffering and dying to the freedom of new life. Know that I am with you in your journey of obedience for I have gone before you in that same journey. My blessing to you this night gives you strength.

June 17, 1993
Message from Our Lady

My dear little children, praise be Jesus! My little ones, as many of you leave to return to your homes know that I leave with you. And to you my little ones who remain, I remain with you here. I am your Mother of Joy. I am the same mother who was and who is. I am your mother. As my Son is your Jesus Who was and Who is, He also is here with you, to be with you always no matter where you are. He remains with you. He is your Jesus of Mercy. My little, little children, know that your prayers are so much needed because of the power of salvation which frees many souls. Never cease praying. Always unite in love and unity daily. MY JESUS AWAITS YOUR PRAYERS AND YOUR LOVE. NEVER FORGET HOW MUCH YOU ARE LOVED. I thank you, my children, for taking seriously my call to prayer and unity. Pray daily with all your heart and do not fear. I AM HERE AND I AM HERE AS MY SON IS HERE. HE IS MERCY AND LOVE. Bless you, my little ones, and thank you for responding to my call. Peace.

June 17, 1993
Message from Our Lord

My dear ones, I come this night to reassure you that I do listen to what you say to Me. Through all of the words of your mouth I look first into your heart. My dear ones, never fear to ask, never fear to speak because through your words you will eventually give Me your heart. I tell you again I do listen. I do hear every word, and I present you each time you pray to My heavenly Father. I love you! Know that I love you. Your prayers do not go unanswered because they do not go unlistened to. My Father answers your prayers within your heart. Listen with your heart and you will hear Us speak to you. We speak to your heart in peace and in mercy. I love you! I listen! We answer!

June 24, 1993
Message from Our Lady

My dear ones, I come this night to encourage you to follow the example of John. Be courageous speaking and living the truth no matter what the cost. John preceded my Son. He spoke the truth, he lived the truth, and in that he was joy filled and proclaimed the glory of God. Follow the example of John. Allow my Son to increase within you, allow Him to be your all. I love you, my dear ones, my dear little ones. I give you my love this night and I bless you and take your hearts with mine to the heart of my Son. We are always with you as you live the truth, as you speak the truth, as my Son increases within you.

July 15, 1993
Message from Our Lord

My dear ones, I invite you again this night to truly come to Me with all of your heart. Come to Me in My word; come to Me in the Eucharist of My love; come to Me in the quiet of your heart. As you do, I will comfort you; I will give you peace; I will heal you.

Come! Do not wait. Come! I love you. Come to Me! I will never disappoint you. Come to Me so that My mercy may be poured out upon you. It is I, My dear ones, who has been sent by My Father to refresh you, to encourage you, to save you. But you need to come to Me. I am with you. Do not be distracted or led astray. Come! I bless you and give you the grace of My healing this night. I speak to your heart My word of love.

July 22, 1993
Message from Our Lord

My dear ones, I, your Lord, invite you this night to come to Me so that I may make you into a new person. Bring Me all of your failings, all of your sins - your sins for which I died; for I wish to heal you, and forgive you, and restore your innocence. My dear ones, do not hold on to your sins. Hold on to Me! Allow Me to make you into a new creation as I present you to My Father who is your Father. I love you, My dear ones. Come to Me and I will restore your innocence. I bless you this night with My mercy, and My healing, and My grace.

July 29, 1993
Message from Our Lord

My dear ones, My Father and I and Our Holy Spirit have been with you from the very beginning. My Father sends Me now again to you to remind you that We are still with you, Father, Son and Spirit. This night I invite you to be with Us, to be conscious of Us with you every moment of every day. It saddens My heart, My dear ones, when I see you acting as if you were alone, as if you were orphans. Be with Us in thought, and in action; in attitude and in spirit. The strength that My Father will give you, the grace that comes from Our Spirit and the mercy that I long to give you is waiting for you. Accept these gifts and live in unity with Us. I love you. I am still with you. My Father is with you and Our Spirit abides within you. I bless you this night with My real presence. Peace.

August 5, 1993
Message from Our Lady

My dear little ones, I, your mother, come to you this night to invite you to look again at my Son, Jesus. To follow Him truly is to take up your cross, to sacrifice, and to suffer whatever comes as you follow Him. Little ones, so many times it is tempting to separate the cross from your life. Separating the cross from your life is separating yourself from my Son. Know that He is with you in your suffering. He is with you as you carry your cross, and it is only through your cross that you will reach Heaven. Remember this, little ones, when you face each day what my Son asks of you. Know that He has sent me to you. Know that I am with you, that I pray with you and for you. I love you and I take you in my arms and present you to my Son. Do not be afraid of the cross, my dear little ones. It is the sign of your victory because it is the sign of my Son's victory. Live in His peace and know that I love you.

September 2, 1993
Message from Our Lord

My dear ones, I come this night to remind you that I, your Lord, am always with you. I ask you again to trust in Me and in My Father Who is your Father. Trust, My dear ones, especially in those times when the situations in your life seem impossible or overpowering, I am with you. I will never abandon you. As you trust you allow Me to bring more of the gifts that I wish to give. This night, My dear ones, I again bless you with My spirit, with peace and with courage, with healing and with My mercy. Trust, trust! I am with you.

September 9, 1993
Message from Our Lady

My dear little ones, I come this night to encourage you to listen to my Son. Know that forgiveness and love go hand-in-hand. Know also that these are very difficult to live. My Son calls us to the narrow way; to the way of His light and His truth; to the way which truly will cause suffering to us, not because of what He asks but because of the resistance of the world. When you are loving and forgiving then you are full of my Son's peace. The world does not understand and there are those in the world who will hate you for loving, for living a life of forgiveness. I am with you through this each step of your way. My dear, dear little ones, know that my Son, our Lord Jesus, truly is your way and my way to God Our Father. In His name this night I bless you. Know that we love you and although His way is narrow and sometimes difficult, you are not alone. Be at peace my dear children. I am your mother!

September 16, 1993
Message from Our Lady

Praise be my Son, Jesus, your Saviour. O my little ones, the grace of God is upon you. My dear, dear children, I need your prayers. I need your prayers desperately for peace in this world; for the salvation of mankind through love and kindness. These days, my little ones, there is so much evil. Satan does not want those that are with him, but he wants those who wish to follow the way of my Son. He wishes to molest them. He wishes to cause great devastation through destruction and division. Days of great division are coming, days in which many in the world will choose not to walk with my Son.

I wish for all to return back to God. Little ones, please unite in prayer, in harmony and in love. Through kindness and through love you will conquer the world; for my Son has conquered the world. My Son is with you.

My little ones, I love you and I know you can love, love far beyond the surface, love deep to the core. Be strong, take courage,

courage in Jesus. Look into your heart and rest in my Son. Know I am with you. Know my Son loves you tremendously and it is because of Him you ARE. Try, my little ones, you must try. Fight with all your being to return back to the good ways, the simple ways, the loving ways. Love one another and then my Son will know how deeply you love Him. Bless you, my little ones, and thank you for responding to my call. Peace.

September 23, 1993
Message from Our Lady

My dear little children, praise be Jesus! My little ones, never be afraid. Do not fear. My Son is with you always. Live in simplicity and love. Pray for peace and love to dwell in your hearts at all times. Pray to be adopted by those in Heaven to intercede for you through peace and through love. You are little children, and you are very much loved by my Son and many. Do not fear for what is now happening in your lives, but look to the true happiness of your TRUE life in eternal bliss, and be at peace through love.

God has His hand upon you. He has graced you. Return to simple ways of thoughts, prayers and actions, and you will live in His peace of His love. You are so special, my little ones. It is the evil one trying to cause confusion and division. Remember, Jesus is gentle and tender and kind, AND YOU ARE HIS. HE LOVES YOU AND WILL NEVER FORGET YOU, even though others may forget you. He is your hope, your ONLY hope. Return back to Him. Bless you, my little ones. Thank you for responding to my call.

September 23, 1993
Message from Our Lord

I invite you to go deep within your heart, and there to listen to Me speaking to you. There in the innermost recesses of your heart you will find and discover who I AM for you, and what I want for you. Each of you is precious to Me. I love you. It is My desire to grace you from your innermost being, so that you may truly be free

161

as the sons and daughters of My Father. Pray, My dear ones, to enter into your heart. I dwell there because of Our Holy Spirit. Be at peace. I give you again this night My peace, My strength. Know that I am with you. Allow Me to truly be your Lord.

September 30, 1993
Message from Our Lady

My dear little children, praise be Jesus! My little ones, put aside all worries and anxieties, and give your love totally to My Son. Love Him. He wants all of you. Ask Him to remove your wandering thoughts and doubts, so that you can give yourself totally to Him. Simply love Him, praise Him, and just be with Him. He awaits your love. He desires you.

Please, my little ones, there is much devastation in this world, and it is very important that you tend to Jesus. Accept His will and trust in His goodness. Do not allow the evil one or his companions to torture you interiorly. Be free in my Son by putting aside any anxiousness, and love Him. He will grant you His peace. Call on your angels for assistance. I bless you, my little ones. Thank you for responding to my call.

October 7, 1993
Message from Our Lady

My dear little children, praise be Jesus! This night, my little ones, I want you to know that freedom can only come by living the truth. Know, my children, that the way you live, your moral values, and your love will be the deciding factor to being free. Live the truth of God set by His word, His commandments. Be free interiorly and exteriorly. Be obedient to my most beloved Pope. Do not turn from him. He has outlined the way to freedom. He has outlined the truth. I love you, my little ones; and I come to tell you that many of your moral values are not the way of truth, the way of my Son. To be free you must live in His truth.

Please pray the rosary. Many graces come from the rosary and with my Son's grace you will be guided to live in His truth, and you will be protected. My Son will grace you in changing to live His goodness, if you are willing and open to knowing the truth. The truth will challenge you and lead you to freedom, peace, happiness and holiness. Bless you, my little ones, and thank you for responding to my call.

October 7, 1993
Message from Our Lord

My dear little ones, so often I see that you ask but then also you tell Me what to give you. So often I see you seeking, but then again you tell Me what you are looking for. So often you knock, but only on the door that you already know. My dear ones, I have told you only to ask, to seek, and to knock. Allow My Father and yours to give what He sees is best for you. I love you. And so often I see you not allowing My Father to give what he wants. My narrow minded children, do you think that God is as limited as you? I am here this night to ask you not to limit the power of God in your life. He would do so much more for you and through you if you would allow it.

My dear ones, listen to me this night - change your attitude and, if need be, even the way of your prayer. You constantly are looking for freedom. I, your Jesus, ask you to give God, My Father, and your Father, freedom to act in your life as He wants to. Then you will truly be free; you will truly be joyful; you will truly be peaceful; and then will your prayers truly be answered. I give you My peace and My mercy this night. I bless you and love you.

October 14, 1993
Message from Our Lady

My dear little children, praise be Jesus! My little ones, please do not despair. Have hope and live in faith and in my Son's love, and in His fidelity. Please my little ones, focus on prayer and practice my Son's words through love. Pray; rejoice in His greatest gift in the Mass; study His word and be committed to following His way. It is time to remain faithful to your commitments of prayer. Do not replace your prayer time with other options. There is only one priceless option - that of your desire to pray and to be with my Son. He will grace you, my little ones, with abundant virtues if you remain committed to Him, allowing Him to challenge you to growth. I love you, my little ones, and bless you in His name. Please take the time for prayer and study His word. Do not lose sight of your focus on Him. Thank you for responding to my call, a priceless calling to prayer and love.

October 14, 1993
Message from Our Lord

My dear ones, I come this night from My Father who sends Me to remind you again of His love. He has shown you His love through Me, through My life, through My death, and as I was raised up by Him, through My resurrection. Now he sends Me again. And again I willingly come to encourage you to listen more closely to what God is saying to you, what My Father has said through Me - keep His commandments as I kept His commandments. Be faithful to Him. My dear ones, persevere on your journey. Do not allow fatigue to overcome you. Know that I am with you. I know it is not easy, but with Me each step can be filled with joy. Listening and faithfulness will strengthen you as you continue. Bless you with the mercy of My heart and the love of My Father, Who is your Father. Amen!

October 28, 1993
Message from Our Lady

My dear little children, praise be Jesus! My little ones, know that Jesus in His infinite mercy is gently molding you. When you struggle with interior pain, it is difficult to realize how gracious Jesus is in allowing the many things of yourself to surface. It is because of His love that He promotes healing through your pain. Self-abandonment and detachment are necessary but are also unending struggles for you. Know, my little ones that spiritual freedom can surface from your struggles. It is your purity of intention and your openness that will allow divine providence to victoriously ensue. Continue to pray, my little ones, and allow God's will to be done. Do not fight interior cleansing. In order to live in union with Him you must die on one level only to be reborn on another.

I bless you, my little ones. I am with you and love you. God loves you. Do not fight His love by trying to control. Rest in Him. Be at peace. Do not keep your distance. Jesus loves you. Thank you for responding to my call.

October 28, 1993
Message from Our Lord

My dear ones, as I called My apostles I am calling you this day at this time. As I called each of them from their different and varied works and labors and lives, I call you, all of you, who are children of My Father, from your varied and different works and labors and ways of lives. But there is a difference, My dear ones, I call you not to come out of your different ways of lives, not to leave your different tasks or labors, but rather to stay where you are and to work and labor, showing those around you that God is the center of your life. This is the way My Father and I, and Our Holy Spirit will touch and transform the lives of many. You will not be alone for I will be with you. Our Spirit will be guiding you. I encourage you to use the gifts that My Father has given to you where you are at this moment to touch those around you. This is the kind of apostle I call you to be. I love you and I bless you this night with My strength and My courage, My mercy and My peace.

November 4, 1993
Message from Our Lord

My dear ones, I am with you this night to tell you that you, who are children of God, are judging one another. My dear ones, I ask you - who made you judge over anyone? There is but one judge and that has been given to Me by My Father. My dear ones, do not be self-righteous. Look down on no one. Pray instead for those you are concerned for. I look into your hearts and I see so much judgment, so much selfishness. My dear ones, please do not judge lest you be judged. I give you the grace that you need to pray, not to judge. I give you the grace to be simple humble children of God My Father and yours. Be those children. Love simply. Embrace the truth. As you do these things you will not have time to judge others. I challenge you this night to listen to My words and to put them into practice so that you may give honor and glory to God. I love you and I am with you always. I bless you this night with My peace and with My mercy.

November 18, 1993
Message from Our Lord

My dear ones, I come this night to tell you again of the love of My Father. This is the time of a great visitation during which many graces are bestowed upon you if you listen and respond. My dear ones, you do know the way to peace. It is simply to follow the commandments of My Father and your Father; to follow what I have asked of you and what I have given you through the example of My life. Take courage. Accept the strength which I give you through My spirit. Know that I am with you; that My mother walks with you, that Our holy angels surround you to protect you. Know that I speak the truth to you. As you follow this way of peace, you will be, and already are, light to the world. Again, I say take courage and continue, persevere and follow in My command. I bless you this night with the grace that you most need. I give you My mercy and My healing.

December 2, 1993
Message from Our Lord

My dear ones, I want you to know again this night I am with you always. When you cannot see Me, when you cannot feel Me and even when you cannot hear Me, I am with you. I thank you for your persevering prayer. I thank you for your love of My Father, of Me, of Our Holy Spirit, and of My mother. I bless you, My dear ones, this night with My merciful peace and with My joy that is beyond your understanding. Know that I am with you.

December 16, 1993
Message from Our Lord

My dear ones, this night I come to encourage you to continue on your journey. You know I am with you every step of the way. I have said this to you so often. I encourage you now to believe what I say, to continue in courage this journey of yours. My dear ones, I so often see, though, there is so little joy within you. Yours is the best of all joy. You are God's children. You are redeemed by My blood. This is the cause of your joy. This is the reality of joy; and yet so often I see so little joy within you. And so this night I say to you: "Be joyful children of God." Know that you are not alone. Know that you are strengthened through Our Holy Spirit. Know that I continue to send to you My mother who prays for you daily. I bless you, My dear ones, with My peace. I again share with you the joy of God.

December 23, 1993
Message from Our Lady

My dear children, be at peace. Be at peace. For it is the peace of my Son that I bring to you this night. As you receive Him this night, you receive the Prince of Peace, who is born upon the altars of the world every day so that He can be born within your hearts and souls everyday. I ask you to prepare for Him everyday. Receive Him ev-

167

eryday in His Eucharistic presence. My Jesus, the King of Kings, comes to you each day in this humblest of forms. Can you not prepare each day to receive Him with the same fervor you prepare for His birth? My little ones, my Jesus comes to you each day to fill you with His peace, His love, His joy. Come and adore Him within the tabernacle of your hearts and souls. I invite you to come each day to the King of all Kings, my Jesus, and allow Him Who is peace to dwell within you, filling you with His Joy and His love. I love you, my sweet children, I love you. Prepare to receive our King. Thank you for having so lovingly responded to my call.

December 30, 1993
Message from Our Lord

My dear ones, I come this night to encourage you to live now in My Kingdom. Abandon the trappings of this world. Live My Kingdom now! My dear ones, there is no need for you to wait. Live now in My Kingdom. Be truly children of God whom you are. Live My peace and My joy. Live My compassion and My mercy. Live daily the love that Our Holy Spirit places within you. Look at each other through My eyes. Look beyond the trappings and see the reality of your life with God. Allow this to be the goal for your new year. As you live more in My Kingdom now, you will truly be in My Kingdom... My Kingdom, through you, can begin when you say yes by the way you live. I bless you at the end of this your year. I give you My strength, and My mercy, and My perseverance as you begin your new year.

January 13, 1994
Message from Our Lady

My dear little children, praise be Jesus! My little, little children, know how precious the gift of family is given from my Son. Always unite in harmony and love your family members. Each person in your family is a special gift to you from God. Each is special in God's love and very important in His eyes. Always unite with each other in your family. It is an important key to salvation. Where there is love there is God. Look beyond your differences and know how God created each one of you in love. See His love in your family and share this love with others in your community. I bless you, my little ones, in the name of my Son, and I pray for your strength to persevere in God's love. Love saves; love heals and love conquers. Love is victory. Love your family. Love God, and thank Him for the many blessings He has bestowed upon you through the family. Peace. Thank you for responding to my call.

January 27, 1994
Message from Our Lord

My dear ones, I ask you this night to again listen to Me speaking to you; not only in this way here in this place, but in My sacred scriptures, in My Most Blessed Sacrament and within your heart. In the innermost urgings of your heart it is I; know that. Be assured of that. I do not leave you orphan. I give you My faith and Our Holy Spirit, and I, Myself, am with you. Even in the dark times I am there. Step out in faith as you listen to Me. Do not be timid, but brave. I am with you, but My dear ones, if you do not listen to Me you will listen to other voices which will lead you from Me. Listen and you will hear. Trust and you will understand. This night I bless you again with My mercy, and give you the courage to continue in perseverance in your journey.

February 3, 1994
Message from Our Lord

My dear ones, I ask you this night to listen to Me. My dear ones, because of the gift My Father has given, I have overcome the world. I ask you again to listen. I have overcome, through the gracious mercy of My Father, all that you are struggling with, even your sin. Listen, My dear ones, I give you My mercy. I give you My love. I give you My consolation. My dear ones, please accept these gifts. Do not be consumed with your sin; with your anxiety.

Come to Me; come to your understanding Lord; come to the One Who has died for you; come to the One Who is raised to new life for you. Accept My love for you; accept the gift of redemption within My love and you will be in the light of the Son of God, and you will reflect the love and the joy, and the hope, and the peace that My Father offers you.

My dear ones, I AM WITH YOU NOW AND ALWAYS! Listen! Listen! I bless you again this night for your journey. Trust in Me. I will never disappoint you. I will give you all you need!

February 17, 1994
Message from Our Lord

My dear ones, I come to you this night to encourage you to choose life, the life which My Father and Our Holy Spirit give to you. This life, My dear ones, can only truly be lived if you die to your selfishness. This life to be fully lived needs to come from embracing your cross. To the world, this is folly. To the world, this is meaningless but, My dear ones, the world does not know what true life is. This night I strengthen you so that you may carry the cross of your daily lives and so that you may embrace it. I have given you the example, and I have shown you where the cross leads. It leads to eternal life, life to its fullest measure. There is nothing to fear. Even your weakness and unwillingness can be overcome, if you give those to Me. I love you and I encourage you during this time to choose life by embracing your cross. You are not alone. I am carrying it with you. I bless each of you this night with My mercy and My love. Be at peace, My dear ones, be at peace!

March 3, 1994
Message from Our Lord

My dear ones, I am with you again this night to remind you that I come under the title of Jesus of Mercy, not justice. I wish to give you My mercy. My dear ones, I ask you to accept the gift of My mercy in your life, for none of you could withstand the justice of My Father. NOW is the time of mercy. I encourage you - respond to this gift. Come to Me with all of who you are and I will heal you, and forgive you, and comfort you. My mercy is for you and for all who allow this gift to be in their hearts. My Father is not stingy with this gift He gives to you through Me. In turn, My dear ones, I encourage you to be generous in your mercy toward others. You block My mercy when you are unmerciful. Look again at each other and see the dear child of God which each of you is. I bless you this night with My peace. I take from you this night your fear. I love you with My mercy this night.

March 10, 1994
Message from Our Lord

My dear ones, I come to you this night to make again a request. Stay close to Me! Come near Me! You need My protection more than you know. Try not to stray and be diluted and disheartened by transitory happiness. My dear ones, the further you are from Me, the weaker you become and the more a prey you are to the evil one. Stay close to Me. I am your strength. My Father has given Me to you, and I have laid down My life for you. Stay close! Allow Me to be your strength and your protection. I love you, and it saddens Me when you hurt yourself by allowing the temptations to overcome you. My dear, dear ones, please do not think that you can walk this journey alone. Do not think that you can take on the evil one by yourself. Stay close to Me and then the fear will leave you and be replaced by My peace. This peace I give you this night along with My healing mercy. I AM WITH YOU ALWAYS! BE WITH ME ALWAYS!

March 17, 1994
Message from Our Lord

My dear ones, I am here with you this night to encourage you to live in faith the words that I speak to you, the words that are truly of My Father, the words that will resonate within your very heart. Live these words, live this faith and be the example and the light to those I send into your life. My dear ones, faith is not knowledge. Faith is believing the word of someone else. Believe the words that I speak. They will give you eternal life; they will give you peace; they will give you My strength. Come to Me, and I will refresh you. Come to Me. I will heal you. Come to Me and receive the forgiveness that is yours. My dear ones, do not wander aimlessly away from Me. Keep close to Me. I will give you life. I bless you this night with the peace of My Father and of Our Holy Spirit. Take courage, My dear ones, take courage!

April 14, 1994
Message from Our Lord

My dear ones, know that I come in love this night to you. As you celebrate My resurrection in your heart, I encourage you to listen to the truth. Listen to Our Holy Spirit speaking to your heart. Listen to My living word in the scripture and be permeated with the truth of Myself in the Eucharist. The truth, My dear ones, will sometimes be very difficult for you to listen to for it will require of you change; it will require of you abandonment. It will require of you true humility. Know that I speak the truth of My Father to all and this truth touches each person's heart, but it is up to each one to respond or not. I ask you this night to listen to the truth and to respond. There are many who disguise their lives with half truths. My dear ones, you need not be afraid of these people. I encourage you simply to come before Me in My Most Blessed Sacrament There you will know what is true and what is false. Know that your Risen Lord - know that I am with you in a very special way during these days. Take advantage of this time, My dear ones. I bless you this night with My peace and My mercy. Know that I take you, each of you, to My heart in love.

April 21, 1994
Message from Our Lord

My dear ones, I am here again tonight with you to encourage you to continue in your journey. Know that I am with you, that I, Myself, through My Eucharist, am your food for the journey. Know with all of your hearts that it is truly I, your Lord, in the Eucharist, truly present with you, and to you, and for you always. I am with you always; and in this gift of Myself to you I show My love and My constancy. I invite you ever closer to Me in My Eucharist. Feed upon Me, become one with Me, and I will truly give you rest, and peace, and joy. In My Eucharist, I am your strength. I bless you this night, each of you, with My mercy and My love.

April 28, 1994
Message from Our Lord

My dear ones, I come to you this night to warn you against pride. Pride wars against My very presence within you. My dear ones, I encourage you this night to follow the example that I have set for you, that My mother has set for you. Beware of spiritual pride. Know with all of your hearts, My dear ones, that without the love of My Father you could do nothing. My dear ones, in humility and honesty before God you will please Him. In humility you will honor Him. Through humility will you attract others to Him. My dear ones, please know that I can truly walk with you only when you are humble. When you are full of pride you walk alone. Come to Me; learn from Me; listen to Me, and you will be pleasing to My Father. I bless you this night, My dear ones, with the grace to open your eyes and to see the ways in which you walk in pride. I give you also the strength to now walk humbly with your God.

May 12, 1994
Message from Our Lord

My dear ones, I come to you on this day in which you celebrate My Ascension, to assure you to be joyful, for I am coming to you again. It is I, your Lord, Who is coming to you. My dear ones, you do not have to wait, however, until I come at the end of your world; for I come to you daily, if you allow it. I walk every minute with you. I am with you in My Eucharist. I am with you in My word. I am with you in My Most Blessed Sacrament.

My dear ones, I am always coming to you. Never forget My presence with you, and as I did with My disciples of old, I do with you this night, My disciples of now — I send you into your world to be My instruments of peace, of mercy, of love, of joy, of truth, of compassion, and above all, at this time, be My disciples of hope. Preach these gifts not by your words but with your life. Know that I give you My strength and that I am coming to you each moment, if you allow Me to. Open your hearts and receive Me. I give you My peace, dear ones, and the grace of perseverance. I love you!

May 26, 1994
Message from Our Lord

My dear ones, as I come to you this night through the grace of God Our Father, I extend My mercy to you. I invite you now in the quiet of your heart to answer this question, a question that I asked the blind beggar long ago. As I ask this question of you and as you answer in your heart, I assure you I am listening as I listened to him, and so I ask each of you, 'What do you wish Me to do for you?' (A long pause followed). As I said to him so long ago I say to each of you this night - you may leave this place in My peace, your faith is making you whole. My mercy, My dear ones, is the gift that I give to you. It is through My mercy and through your being merciful to others that you will be healed from that which is keeping you from Me. Know that I am with you, that I wish you to be whole, and that I love you. Live in My peace!

June 9, 1994
Message from Our Lord

My dear ones, I, your Lord, come to you this night to invite you to seek the holiness that My Father and Our Spirit and I wish to give you. Our holiness that We wish to give is unlike the holiness of the world. It is even unlike the holiness that you may be seeking. Do you not yet understand, My dear ones, that God's ways are not yours? Why do you continue to try to figure out what will happen? Trust, trust! Have I not died for you? Are you not precious in the sight of My Father? Have We not sent you Our Spirit? Why do you still insist on being anxious? This anxiousness blocks the holiness that We wish to give you. Listen to Me now. Allow this word to be your point of reflection in front of My most Blessed Sacrament. The word is this - SIMPLICITY! Come as a simple child and you will receive the holiness of God. I bless you this night; and I give you My courage to be simple, holy children of My Father.

June 16, 1994
Message from Our Lord

My dear ones, I am here with you again this night as your Lord and Saviour to plead with you. Listen to what I have asked, to what My mother continues to ask. Rededicate yourself, each of you, to prayer. You have become, My dear ones, so scattered. Come again before Me in My most Blessed Sacrament. Come to Me in that precious gift of Mine and My Father's, and Our Spirits to you. I see within your hearts and there is such a lack of forgiveness. My dear ones, look upon the crucifix. Remember what I have done for you. Imprint that picture within your mind. Press it to your heart and then see how terrible it is when you refuse to forgive yourself. I have died for you. Isn't that proof that you are forgiven? Come to Me through the sacrament of reconciliation and receive again My healing and My forgiveness. My dear ones, your lack of forgiveness of yourself blocks the mercy, and the joy, and the peace that I wish to give to you. Come to Me. Present yourself again to Me in

175

My most Blessed Sacrament. I want with all of My heart to heal you, to strengthen you. With My strength you will forgive yourself, and so this night I bless you with the strength that you need, with the courage of My Holy Spirit. You again, this night, as you come to Me, can be a new creation. Be at peace now. Fear is useless.

June 23, 1994
Message from Our Lord

My dear ones, I am with you this night to again remind you that My mercy and the mercy of My Father and of Our Holy Spirit is with you, all of you, and each of you, always. You will not understand the bounds of My mercy. I ask you simply to accept this gift. As in the days of Zechariah, the mercy of God was so great that it seemed to him as impossible. Look what God's mercy can do! My dear ones, it is you who block the mercy of God. Allow God to be Who He is. Allow Me to truly be your Saviour and allow Our Holy Spirit to truly overwhelm you. You have no idea of what God's mercy can do. Please do not limit My mercy.

June 30, 1994
Message from Our Lord

My dear ones, I, who have died for your sins, come this night to remind you that the healing that each of you needs the most is to be healed of your sin. My dear ones, sin is truly the cancer of the soul. Come to Me for healing of your sinfulness. Come, allow Me to forgive you. Know, My dear ones, that as you carry your sin you become more burdened, My joy cannot be within you, My peace is disrupted, and there is so much confusion and anxiety within. Please allow Me to forgive you. I am the Saviour of your soul. My prayer to My Father is that you stop sinning. Do not kill the life of Our Spirit within you with your sin. Receive and celebrate the great sacrament of reconciliation; and allow Me to forgive and to heal you. Know, My dear ones, that My spirit within you is more powerful than the spirit of evil which tempts you to sin. This night I give you the grace of My mercy to begin again and to walk in innocence and peace. I love you, and this night I take each of you to My heart.

July 7, 1994
Message from Our Lord

My dear ones, I come to you this night to remind you of the gift that My Father and Our Spirit has given to you through Me, your Saviour. It is the gift of mercy, My dear ones. This gift is not given to you for you to hold, but to be given through you to others. Truly, what you have been given, give as a gift. I encourage you to learn the depth of My mercy; the strength, the truth, the compassion, the joy of My mercy. Learn and live this gift. I bless you this night with My courage to accept My mercy, the mercy of your God, and then to live it and to give it to others. Peace, My dear ones. I am with you!

July 14, 1994
Message from Our Lord

My dear ones, I come to you this night, your Lord and Saviour to speak to your heart, to say to you how often you take upon yourself yokes and burdens which are not the ones that I ask you to bear. My dear ones, you are scattered within yourselves. Come back to Me, listen to what I speak to your heart. This will give you comfort and peace, and then go and do what I ask. The anxiety you have is never from Me, but My dear ones, when you take upon yourselves those things which I have not asked you to. This night, I ask each of you to come humbly before Me and to repent of your pride, to repent of those times in which you did not listen, those times in which you did not come to ME before you acted. Present all of this to Me and also the hurt that you have sustained because you have been carrying burdens and yokes which are not of Me. My dear ones, when I ask you to carry a burden, I am there to carry it with you. My yoke chafes only when you go from Me and try to do on your own what you decide to do. Come back to Me so that you may be renewed in joy and in peace. I bless you, My dear ones, this night again with My merciful love. Listen to Me.

July 21, 1994
Message from Our Lord

My dear ones, I am here again with you this night to speak again plainly to you and not in parables. Each of you is chosen by My Father and so I call you friends. Listen to Me. Know that your Father, My Father, loves you incomparably, unendingly. Know that I love you; that I have given My life for you. I have shown you the way of salvation. My dear ones, you have nothing to fear. You are God's children. I am always with you. Know that My strength is within you. I bless you this night as I remind you that you are never alone. Be encouraged, My dear ones, as you continue your journey. I am with you every step of the way. Peace. I give you this night the blessing of My mercy.

August 11, 1994
Message from Our Lord

My dear ones, I come to you this night to remind you again of My presence here with you; to remind you again of My presence within your hearts; to remind you again that I am with you always. I know, My dear ones, that as you look upon this world the power of evil is so overwhelming. You are forgetting that I have overcome this world. Your heads are so turned with spectacular events. My dear ones, I am here to remind you what is of importance is never seen by the human eye. It is the miracle of change and conversion that is worked within your heart, if you allow Me to be there with you. As you allow that conversion, you will not not be so overwhelmed and over-awed by spectacular happenings. You will know the truth and so you will be truly free. This night I tell you that the road to true freedom within Me is forgiveness. It is the key to the Kingdom of God, and so this night, My dear ones, I, Who have paid the price of your redemption with My very blood, bless you with strength to forgive. Accept My blessing and live in the freedom of God.

Thursday, September 29, 1994
Message from Our Lady

My dear children, I your Mother of Joy, rejoices with you this night along with all the angels and saints! Tonight, especially this night, I ask you to always call on the angels for guidance and protection. This is a time of much warfare and I ask that you call on my beloved Archangel Michael to defend you. He will always be there, my little ones, along with me, covering you with my mantle of love. Never cease praying, my little children.

I love you and I thank you for responding to my call.

Thursday, October 27, 1994
Message from Our Lady

It is I, your mother, who come to be with you this night. My dear ones, reach out in love. Do not judge. You do not know the deepest intentions of your brothers and sisters. Pray to continue to love and to think well of each other.

I am always with you, my little ones. I do not judge you. I love you.

Pray with all of your heart. Peace to you.

Thursday, November 3, 1994
Message from Our Lady

My dear ones, I ask you again this night to pray for my Jesus' mercy. My little ones, it is *truly* there for the taking. My Son loves you so much and wants to pour His mercy upon you. Pray, my dear ones. Pray for abundant graces of His mercy. He wants to shower you with His love.

Open your hearts this night to my Son's love and mercy.
I love you dearly, My little ones. We are right here by your side.

Thursday, December 15, 1994
Message from Our Lord

My dear ones, I speak to you this night, words to your heart. The prophets have given Me the title "Emmanuel." I come this night to remind you that I am with you. My dear ones, I have never abandoned you and I never will. You need not be afraid. Give Me again your heart. Allow My grace in your life to heal and strengthen you, and to light again the fires of our Holy Spirit within you.

During these days I am closer to you than your very self. I am your hidden Lord. Know that I can be found within the innermost part of your heart. I love you! My dear ones, I love you so much that I became one with you, one of you. I came for you. Listen during these next days to Me speaking to your heart. I indeed have something to say to each of you. Open to Me and listen.

I bless you this night again with My mercy, and My strength, and My healing.

Thursday, December 22, 1994
Message from Our Lord

My dear ones, this night I present to your heart My Mother. Know that she is your example of faithfulness to God as she was My example on earth. Know that My Father and Our Holy Spirit were able to do great things for her and through her for the world because of her humility. She was and is open to My Father's will. She abandoned all of her personal wills, and plans, and desires so that God's plan, and will, and desire can be effective through her. My Mother is the holy one through which I was given to you. I encourage you, my dear ones, to follow her example to allow God to so possess you that His joy, and mercy, and love can become a reality again within this world.

My dear ones, she it is who is crushing the head of the serpent, and when you unite your heart with hers, then My father can use you also to bring salvation to the world. I bless you this night with My grace and with the strength of Our Holy Spirit, the same Spirit that strengthened and still strengthens My Mother. I love her with all of My heart. I encourage you to love her as I do.

Thursday, December 29, 1994
Message from Our Lord

My dear ones, I have been sent to you by My Father as your light. During these days there are so many different kinds of lights which can be so distracting for you. My light shines within your heart. Look there, and do not be blinded or distracted by the lights of this world. They promise you everything, and give you nothing. I promise you life forever, and that I give you even now. If you look within your heart and allow the love that I offer you to grow, then even now you will be living within My kingdom.

Oh, my dear ones, I know that it is not easy to live what I have asked, especially when you are ridiculed; and when it seems as if the whole world is going away from Me. Let Me assure you, there will always be little ones, like yourselves, who listen and receive My light. You may seem weak, but I give you My strength. I give you My Mother as the example of following My light. I bless you this night, My dear ones. Allow the light of My love and My mercy to shine through you to this world. Live in the way I have asked. Peace be with you.

Thursday, January 12, 1995
Message from Our Lord

I give you this night My peace, and with that gift, I touch each of you and I soften your heart. Peace, my dear ones.

My dear ones, I ask you this night to guard against hardening your hearts. It is so very easy and it happens so quickly that your hearts become hardened once again. My dear ones, you harden your hearts not only by your sins, but also when you become discouraged; when you become anxious; when you become worried; when you are judgmental; when you gossip; when you fear. So many times each day your heart becomes hardened. I ask you, my dear ones, allow Me to heal your hardened hearts. I truly will to heal you. Many times a day, as often as it takes, present your hardened heart to Me and I will again soften your heart. No matter how many times I will heal you, but know that it is so easy for your heart to become hardened, and then proud, and it paralyzes you. My dear ones, you are not alone. Take seriously what I say. Listen to Me, and if you cannot hear Me within your heart, ask Me to heal you because your heart has become hardened once again. Pray, my dear ones, because prayer is the gift that softens the hardest heart.

Thursday, February 2, 1995
Message from Our Lord

My dear ones, on this Feast of My Presentation I come to you to give you an invitation. I invite you to follow My example, and to allow My Mother to present you to God as she presented Me. What a great service she provided for Me when I was helpless, when in My humanity I could not present Myself. She took Me in her loving arms, carried Me to the temple, and did for Me what I was unable to do. My dear ones, so often because of your weakness, because so often you are overcome by so much sin, oftentimes that you are not even aware because your hearts are numb. In those times allow My Mother to take you in her loving arms and to do for you what you cannot. Allow her to present you to God. I love My Mother and I thank God for her who did for Me what I could not do. She is your mother. I gave her to you. Allow Her, my dear ones, to present you to God and in that offering of yourself you will then be given what you need, through her intercession, in her loving arms.

I bless you this night and I give to you, each of you, a greater love for her who has given all to God. If this world would allow her she would present the whole world to God. Peace, my dear ones. I love you.

Thursday, February 16, 1995
Message from Our Lord

My dear ones, I ask each of you this night what I asked My disciples, "Who do you say that I am?", but I ask you, my dear ones, in another way this night. Does your attitude tell the world who I am for you? Does the way you live your life speak about who I am for you? My dear ones, I thank you for your response, but I ask you to increase your effort in changing your attitudes, in changing your preconceptions. I ask you to stop judging others. I ask you, my dear ones, to stop judging your God. Allow My Father to do His will within you and within the world. Allow Him to be God. Allow Me to be your Savior and allow Our Holy Spirit to live within you. To do this you need the gift of simplicity not only in your material life but most importantly, my dear ones, in your spiritual life.

I encourage you this night to continue to come before Me in My Blessed Sacrament and learn what simplicity is for you. I bless you, my dear ones. I give you the grace of My mercy and My love. Be at peace and become children of My Father in your simplicity.

Thursday, February 23, 1995
Message from Our Lord

My dear ones, I come to you this night to ask you to live in simplicity but, my dear ones, it is not of worldly simplicity that I speak, or simplicity in material things. I ask you who come here to pray to be simple in your prayer, to be simple in your relationship with Me. I ask you, my dear ones, to come before Me, to listen to Me speak to your heart, to allow Our Holy Spirit to fill you and if you allow this, then you will not go running after complicated spirituality. You will speak simply to Me within your heart. You will pray simple to Me.

I encourage you, my dear ones, to look again at My Mother whom I have given to you. Imitate the simplicity of her prayer. In simplicity you will find peace. I bless you, my dear ones, with My love and My mercy and the grace of My healing.

Thursday, March 2, 1995
Message from Our Lord

My dear ones, I, your Lord, come to you this night inviting you to choose life. My dear ones, do not lose your soul. When you choose sin, you choose death. My dear ones, through My passion and death I freed you. Stay free, my dear ones. Use each moment to choose life: to listen to My words of life; to live as I ask, as My Father asks, as Our Holy Spirit breathes into your heart. Do not choose death. Do not choose to sin any longer. I know you in yourselves are weak. In My own humanity I was weak, but the power of My Father through Our Holy Spirit is your strength, as it was My strength in My humanity.

I bless you this night, My dear ones, with the strength that you need to choose life. Look at Me and not at yourself. Receive My peace this night and the love of My heart.

Thursday, March 16, 1995
Message from Our Lady

My dear little children, I am with you this night, I who am your mother, to remind you that I will take care of you. I will embrace you, my dear ones. I will love you with all my heart. Do not run away from me or from my Son, Jesus, looking for comfort, or love, or consolation in this world. My dear, dear children, this world is passing away. I ask you to allow me to love you and to lead you to my Son. As I have said before, "Am I not here who am your Mother? Are you not in the folds of my garment, in the crossing of my arms, am I not the cause of your joy? Is there anything else you need?"

My dear ones, my dear little children, please believe what I have said to you and what I say to you this night. Wait, wait, on my Son. He is coming and I am sent to you to prepare you. Hold on to me when you are frightened, when you are lonely. I will bring you to Him and my love will fill your heart. In the name of my Son, Jesus, in the name of God Our Father, and in the name of my Spouse, the Holy Spirit, I ask God's blessings upon you now. I love you! Be strong! Don't give up, be strong!

Thursday, March 30, 1995
Message from Our Lord

My dear ones, I come to you this night to remind you that you do hear My voice. You hear it within your heart, and if you do not hear it then your heart is hardened. I say to you as was said before - "harden not your heart." Take your heart to My Mother and allow her with her love to soften your heart, and then you will hear Me again. My dear ones, I love you and I draw you near to Me as a shepherd does his sheep. You will recognize My voice. Listen to My call and follow Me. There is no need of fear. I am with you. During these penitential days offer to God Our Father your very life and know that He will give you eternal life. The sufferings of this world are truly, My dear ones, nothing compared to the joy of eternal life.

I bless you this night with My mercy and My peace. Listen to Me!

Thursday, April 27, 1995
Message from Our Lord

My dear ones, I ask you this night to listen and to trust Me. My Father and I, and Our Holy Spirit hear your prayers. You present your needs to Us but then, my dear ones, you don't trust that We hear you. I tell you again this night, your ways are not Our ways and your thoughts are not the thoughts of God. I love you; My Father loves you; Our Spirit is with you. Trust Us! Know that I am with you. Your prayers are heard.

Allow Me, My dear ones, to save you, to work out through you and within you, your good. Have you forgotten that My Father has carved each of you on the palm of His hand? You are not forgotten. My dear ones, do not be sad and do not despair. I am your hope. I hear you. Although you may not be able to see, I see. Although you may not be able to understand - trust. I have your good in My heart.

I embrace you this night, each of you, and encourage you to listen to Me and to trust Me. I bless you with My grace and with My mercy.

Thursday, May 4, 1995
Message from Our Lord

My dear ones, I come to you this night to say again as I said to My disciples so long ago - "I am the Bread of Life!" As you receive Me in My Most Holy Eucharist you become one with Me, and as you become one with Me, you become one with the Father and Our Holy Spirit. We wish to nourish you, my dear ones. Thank you for allowing Us to nourish you; thank you for your adoration; thank you for believing in the reality of Myself within the Eucharist. I tell you it is true what you believe. I am truly present, and when I am present, My Father and Our Spirit are also there. My dear ones, stand firm in your belief. I Am Who I say I Am.

This night I bless you with courage, I strengthen your belief and I say to you your belief is not in vain. You see now with the eyes of faith. Wait — you will see more! I draw all people to Myself in the Eucharist. This is the true miracle of My presence among you. This is how much I love you! (Father Jack's arms are outstretched, then lowered slowly with palms facing congregation.)

Thursday, May 18, 1995
Message from Our Lord

My dear ones, I come to you this night to invite you to live more in My love. To do this, you not only follow My commands but listen to Me speaking to your heart. The new command is love, which means eventually laying down your life. Do you love me enough to lay down your life the way you are living now, and begin to live in the way I will lead you? If you are ready I will lead you, and there will be My joy within you. My dear ones, I ask you to allow Me to lead you; to lead you in ways that you do not understand. In order for you to do this you need to trust Me. And so this night I bless you, each of you, with the gift of My mercy and the gift of trust. Know that you are not alone. Know that I am with you. Peace, My dear ones. Peace.

Thursday, June 8, 1995
Message from Our Lady

My dear little children, I, your Mother, encourage you this night to be single hearted in your love for my Son, and of God Our Father and of the Holy Spirit. With all of who you are, love.

I come to you this night to thank those of you who have said "yes" to the sacrament of marriage. I want you to know, my dear little children, that I am in a special way with you. Know that this is truly a holy vocation. I ask you, both you who are married and you who are not, to pray for those who are married, for those who are preparing for marriage, that their love may be holy and for a noble purpose, not for lust of for taking advantage of each other. My dear little ones, this sacrament of marriage is the sign of God's mercy upon earth. Don't you see that is why the devil wants to destroy this sacrament? Guard against him. Be single hearted in your pursuit of loving God. Focus, my dear little children, on Him and live the vocation to which you have been called. In the name of my Son, Jesus, in the name of God Our Father. and in the name of Their Holy Spirit, I your Mother, bless you this night, and in a special way I am praying for those of you who are married and who are preparing for marriage. I love, my little ones. I love you and I thank you for listening to me. And again as I ask of you so often, I ask this night - do whatever my Son asks. Peace! Peace!

Thursday, June 15, 1995
Message from Our Lord

My dear ones, I come to you this might to encourage you to listen; listen to Our Holy Spirit speak within your heart; listen to the call again to holiness. My dear ones, the more you allow Me to come closer to you, the more I am able to bring My Father and Our Holy Spirit to you also. As We come to you, you will be further and further from this world; from its values; from what it holds sacred. Know that Our holiness is not what the world observes as good.

My dear ones, I give you My courage this night; I give strength to your sagging spirit; I give hope to you; I give you My joy. These gifts lead you on the path of holiness. I bless you, My dear ones, with mercy and with My love.

Thursday, July 13, 1995
Message from Our Lord

My dear ones, this night I come to remind you as My Father reminded Joseph of old that God's ways and plans are not yours. Know that We are with you always, that you are truly loved, and that what may in your sight be tragedy, or defeat, or failure, We can use and do use for good., What you need is trust. I am with you. My Father is with you, and Our Holy Spirit is with you always. Allow Our reign, Our kingdom to grow within you and be dependent upon Us.

I know, my loved ones, that My way is not the way of the world and it is not easy for you. I give you My strength this night to continue on the narrow path; I give you My hope and My encouragement to look toward the Resurrection within you each day; and I give you My mercy and My healing as you go each day through your own passion and death.

I love you, My dear ones, and I bless you this night giving you My peace.

Thursday, July 27, 1995
Message from Our Lord

My dear ones, I come to you this night, your Lord and Savior, to remind you that I speak to you clearly. I have not spoken to you here in parables. I speak to you always the truth in simple language, but not in parables. My dear ones, I ask you this night to again listen to what I have said, to read what I have said in the past to you here. I have said what I have said as a help to you.

Your relationship with God Our Father and with Me, your Savior, and with Our Holy Spirit, does not have to be a complicated one. You, at times, complicate Our relationship, and so I say again - listen to My plain words. There is nothing hidden. Listen with your heart and put into action what I have asked. This will bring you salvation. This will bring you eternal joy with Me. My dear ones, I want a simple relationship with you. Allow that to take place. Know that I love you and that I will never stop speaking to your heart in words that you will understand.

I bless you this night with My mercy and My peace.

Thursday, August 10, 1995
Message from Our Lord

My dear ones, it is true that unless a seed falls into the ground and dies it remains only a seed, but if it dies then it becomes much more. My dear ones, do not be afraid to die to yourself, to your plans, to your dreams. My dear ones, as long as you hold on to your plans, and your hopes, and your dreams. My Father will not be able to fill you and lead you in His plan in My hope for you, and not in dreams but in the reality that is Us. My dear ones, I know that it is a fearful thing for you to let go, but I, your Lord, promise you that I will make you into someone new if you only let go, but you need to let go, you need to die. My dear ones, didn't I give you the ultimate example of what dying brings if we offer ourselves to God Our Father? He made Me new. We will make you new. Unless a grain of wheat falls into the ground and dies, it remains just a grain of wheat! Trust Me when I say to you - "you have no idea what your God has planned for you." Let go and really begin to live. If you accept it this night, I free you now from your fear I heal you from your anxiety and I put within your heart a new hope.

I love you. **I LOVE YOU!!! I LOVE YOU!! If you die to yourself, We will raise you to new life!**

Thursday, September 7, 1995
Message from Our Lord

My dear ones, I want to teach you as I taught My disciples, and so I invite you to come to Me and to listen within your heart as I speak the truth to you. My dear ones, when you sin, it is not I who leave you, it is you who leave Me. I am not put off by your sinfulness. I love you and wish to forgive you and to heal you, but so often I see when you sin you run from Me; you are afraid. My dear ones, do not be afraid of Me. I died for you! I love you. Why do you fear Me? Come to Me when you have sinned so that I may forgive you, and heal you, and strengthen you. With all My heart this night I say again - **I LOVE YOU, I LOVE YOU!** I give you My blessing of peace and of strength this night so that you may not be overcome by your sinfulness. Listen to Me as I speak the truth to your hearts.

Thursday, September 21, 1995
Message from Our Lord

My dear ones, I come to you this night as I came to those so long ago in Matthew's house. I come again to remind you that I wish to give you My mercy. My dear ones, I ask for your honesty. Admit that you need My mercy. Admit that you are sinners, and in that admission, your hearts will be open again to receive the healing that I wish to give you.

Dear ones, you still want both a relationship with Me and to be peaceful in this world. My dear ones, you cannot have both. Choose! You choose by the way you live your life. My dear ones, please listen to Me and not the voices of this world. I encourage you to be faithful even through your sinfulness. I love you. I have given My life for you. I have allowed My blood to be spilled for you. Allow Me to save you. I bless you this night with the grace of My peace; My peace, not the peace that the world gives you; and My peace, My dear ones, will shake the very roots of your soul.

Thursday, September 28, 1995
Message from Our Lord

My dear ones, I come this night to tell you once again that I am with you always. I am with you in each moment of your day. I am with you in the most silent moments of your heart. You are never alone! There is nothing to fear for I am with you. At times, My dear ones, you lose track of Who I Am. Come to Me in My Most Blessed Sacrament and listen as I tell your heart once again Who I Am. I am the One who died for you. I am the One who was nailed to the Cross and hung there for you. I love you and I tell each of you this night as I speak to your heart - I would do it again to save you. I love you. Allow Me to love you. I am here!

I bless you this night with the mercy of My love, and I take each of you as YOU ARE this night in My embrace as I bring you into My heart. Be healed, My dear ones. I will it! Be healed!

Thursday, October 12, 1995
Message from Our Lord

My dear ones, I come this night to remind you, each of you, that Our Father listens to you as He listened and listens to Me. I came to tell you that God was your Father and I say it again to you this night here in this place. You have a Father, you are not orphans. You have a Father Who loves you, Who has loved you so much that He sent Me to you to tell you of His Love, and of His Mercy, of His Forgiveness, of His Healing. And so I remind you this night of His great Love for you. Allow Him, My dear ones, to touch your heart. I say to you as I said many years ago, ask with an open heart and He will receive it. Know with an open mind and all of those things that have caused you doubt or worry, will have the Light of Our Holy Spirit shed upon them. Seek with a merciful heart. Then My dear ones, you will find more than you could have every hoped for. My Father again sends Me to you. This, My dear ones, is His Mercy again to you. **I am your Jesus of God's Mercy.** I bless you with My peace and I grace you with mercy. You are Children of God. You have nothing to fear. Be at peace My dear ones. I am here and I go with you.

Thursday, November 16, 1995
Message from Our Lord

My dear ones, this night I bring you My peace and My serenity for your soul, and for your heart, and for your mind. I assure you this night that you now are already living within My Kingdom because I have placed the seed of My Kingdom within you. As you respond to My invitation to come closer to Me, My Kingdom grows within you. Please, My dear ones, be assured of this. And as you allow My Kingdom to grow within you. My peace will overflow from you to others. You will be full of My joy. You will be instruments of My hope for this world. Do not be disturbed. I am with you now. I will be with you always as I have promised, so there is nothing to fear.

My dear ones, this is true wisdom - to believe in Me, to allow My Father and Our Spirit to dwell within you. This is truly living in the Kingdom of God. And know this - if you do not live in My Kingdom within you here, you will never know My kingdom in heaven.

I give you this night My peace and the serenity of your souls. Know that you are beloved not only of Me, but of My Father and of Our Holy Spirit. Walk in the way of My Kingdom. I love you! I love you and I am with you! Do not fear.

Thursday, December 7, 1995
(8th Anniversary of the Prayer Group)
Message from Our Lady

My dear children, I am here who am your Mother. Children, by the grace of God I am the new Eve. Through the gracious mercy of Him I was chosen. Through His love and Divine providence I was kept safe from the stain of sin from the very first moment of my life. My dear children, I give glory to God for that great gift, and I ask you this night to join me in gratitude to our God for that gift through which the world received my Son, the Savior and Messiah, the Son of God. Give thanks with me this night for that gift of all gifts, **JESUS.** Because of Him, dear children, I am your Mother. He has given me to you and you to me. Come to me. Allow me to love you. Allow me to take you to my Son and into the Heart of God. His mercy, my dear children, is truly without end. I love you. I love you with all of my heart. I will never abandon you. I am with you always because my Son has given me to you. In my very being I proclaim this faithfulness to Him.

I thank you, my dear little ones, my dearest children, for praying; for your faithfulness. I ask you this night to not forget me. I fear if you forget me you will go far from my Son. By the grace of God many of you have listened to me and have allowed me to bring you to my Son, Jesus. Allow this to happen again. Begin again with me this night to glorify God with all of your heart; with all of your soul; with all of your mind; with all of your strength.

I pray for you, my dear ones. I love you. You are my children and I, thanks to God, am your Mother. I hold you, each of you, not only to my heart this night, but I present you to the Heart of my Son, to my Spouse the Holy Spirit, and to God Our Father. Praise Him with Me, my dear ones, praise Him always with me. Peace be with you. Thank you for listening and for responding to the call of My Son.

Thursday, December 14, 1995
Message from Our Lord

My dear ones, I come to you this night to remind you that My Kingdom, the Kingdom of My Father, is within your touch; within the reach of your heart. It is alive in your heart if you allow it to grow there. My dear ones, I know of the many distractions that each of you suffer, those things that tend to pull you away and not to allow you to focus on My Kingdom. Know, My dear ones, that there are many, many kingdoms, but there is only one Kingdom established by My Father. It is not an illusive kingdom - it is truly made for everyone, Sad to say, many choose the other kingdoms.

During this Holy Season allow not only Myself to be reborn within you, but allow God's Kingdom to come alive within you - the Kingdom of Peace and Justice; the Kingdom of Love and Mercy and Peace; the Kingdom of Joy and of Hope. My dear ones, come to Me and I will lead you into God's Kingdom.

I bless you this night with the gift of My Mercy and Peace. Be joyful, My dear ones, and know that I am with you. **I AM EMMANUEL!**

Thursday, January 4, 1996
Message from Our Lord

My dear ones, I come this night to speak to your hearts. I tell you again that I am with you. You celebrate ME at this time as EMMANUEL. I tell you, My dear ones, I AM with you this day and all of the days of your life, I am your Messiah and, if you allow Me, I am your Lord but, My dear ones, I wait on your invitation. Invite Me into your heart. Allow Me truly to be the Lord of your life, and then you will know what true peace is; what overflowing joy is; what hope is. If you only knew how much Our God loves you to have sent Me and to continue to send Me to you. Believe, My dear ones, how much He loves you, and respond in love. Those who truly try to respond in love to God and to each other cannot for long remain in sin. Love conquers sin. I have conquered sin for you.

I love you, My dear ones, and I bless you this night with the gift of My Mercy. Fear not, little ones, you are never alone. I take each of you this night into My Heart. I love you and I give you My Peace.

Thursday, February 1, 1996
Message from Our Lord

My dear ones, I come to you this night to invite you again to turn to Me in your trial; to trust Me. My dear ones, when you look into the future you become fearful. I say to you again, there is truly nothing that you need to fear. Stay with Me in the present. As you look into the future and as you become fearful, I see that you again take control of your lives. My dear ones, I tell you again this night there is only one God. He is My Father and yours. There is only one Jesus. And there is but one Spirit, the Holy Spirit of My Father and Myself. My dear ones, trust Us! Live in the present with Us and you will again be at peace.

I bless you this night, My dear ones, with the grace of My Mercy, the grace of My Peace, and the grace of My Serenity. You are never alone. I walk each step of your journey with you. I bear your cross with you, and if you allow Me, I will share with you My Resurrection! I love you with a love that is everlasting. I take each of you, especially those of you who are most in need of My mercy, into My heart this night where I hold you with all tenderness.

Thursday, February 8, 1996
Message from Our Lord

My dear ones, I come to you this night to ask again that you be single hearted. So many of you have divided hearts. My dear ones, with a divided heart you are handicapped in responding in love to Me, and to My Father, and to the prompting of Our Spirit. Trust Me when I say I love you and when I say I am with you. I invite you again this night to give God your heart as I have given Myself totally in love to My Father. Know that I listen to your hearts but when they are so divided, you do not speak with words of love but with words of fear and anxiety and worry, trying again to take your life in your own hands; trying again to control the future. If you are single hearted, if you truly offer your heart to God, there will be peace My dear ones, for you, and hope and joy that will replace fear and worry, and anxiety and control. I say again this night that I invite you to have a single heart, to be single hearted in your love. I invite you; I do not force you, but I offer you with this single heartedness a way out of your fear, and your worry, and your anxiety. My dear ones, accept please My invitation this night.

I bless you and I am with you always. There is nothing to fear. You, each of you, is in My Heart.

Thursday, February 15, 1996
Message from Our Lord

My dear ones, I come to you this night to ask each of you the same question that I asked My disciples, "Who do you say that I am?" But before you answer, I come to say another thing to you. It is this – you discriminate against Me when you choose sin. You ask Me to wait as you choose to do your will instead of the will of My Father and yours. My dear ones, this discrimination will eventually kill you. I ask you this night to stop discriminating against Me, your Lord; to stop choosing other gods rather than choosing the one true and only God; not to sell your birthright of eternal life for transitory happiness. My dear ones, what you judge as a long life is but an instant before God My Father and yours. Is discriminating against Me worth an eternity of pain, of being away from the God Who created you and Who loves you? Again I ask you to stop this discrimination; to choose again the love that I offer you. In that choice you will answer with all of your heart that I am your Lord and Savior, the Messiah of your soul.

I bless you with peace this night, and I touch each of your hearts with My Mercy which is not only Mine but My Father's and Our Spirit. I love you! Allow Me to love you!

Thursday, February 29, 1996
Message from Our Lord

My dear ones, I come to you this night to ask you again to seek My Father. You look for so many things. You seek after so much, and I see within your hearts so much disappointment and worry, and anxiety. I say to you as I said once before – "seek first the Kingdom of God, His way of holiness, and everything else will be given to you." My dear ones, maybe you don't believe this – that is why I said it again. Truly – seek God's Kingdom within you; His Kingdom of peace and mercy, compassion and hope, and love. When you seek His Kingdom then your prayer will be answered.

My dear ones, stop running so fast within yourself. Take time to allow God's Kingdom to grow within you. During this season of Penance seek Him first. Allow Him to be the King of your heart, and then you will see that you are in need of nothing.

My Father has sent Me to you this night to remind you of His love, and so I bless you this night with His love. I bless you this night with His mercy and I pray for your perseverance. Know that I am with you. There is nothing to fear. Slow down and walk with Me. Walk with Me into His Kingdom.